I'm MAD About YOU

God's Plan for Peace and Harmony When You're Angry at the People You Love

MACK AND BRENDA TIMBERLAKE

CREATION HOUSE
Orlando, FL

Creation House
Strang Communications Company
600 Rinehart Road
Lake Mary, FL 32746
Phone: 407-333-3132
Fax: 407-333-7100
Web site: http://www.strang.com

We would like to dedicate this book to the members and friends of Christian Faith Center, Creedmoor, North Carolina, for their unwavering love and support.

This book is also dedicated to Lillian Laitman, who was superb in assisting us in the editing of the material to complete this book.

CONTENTS

INTRODUCTION

A man approached us for counseling after one of our Double Portion conferences. He was physically, emotionally and spiritually worn out. He began sobbing and told us how he became so obsessed with finding the father he had never known, and as a result he lost everything — his house, his job and, most tragically, his family. He became enraged as he continued to relate his story and with an increasing tone of voice said, "And when I find him, I'm going to ask him, 'Why did you leave me? Why didn't you want me? I wanna be a good father. I don't wanna abandon my son the way you abandoned me.'" Ironically, the very thing he didn't want to happen to his own child occurred because he gave the enemy a foothold by allowing unresolved anger to control him.

As pastors of a congregation of more than five thousand weekly attendees and as conference speakers, we minister to people from every ethnic and socioeconomic background. We have discovered that anger is no respecter of persons. Anger, like anything else, will control you if you don't exercise self-control.

I (Mack) have noticed the problem many men have in dealing with anger. We men sometimes view discussing our frustrations as a sign of weakness instead of a way to strengthen our relationships. As a result, our pent-up anger eventually explodes into a violent action, causing harm to those we love and cherish the most — our families.

Nowhere has violence become more prevalent than in our own country where racial tension, gang-related incidents, spouse and child abuse, and homicides are commonplace. The evening news floods our homes with gloom-and-doom reports of high-profile court cases. When I watch the news, I ask myself, *What causes this man to abuse his wife? Why do the police violently attack a man without a cause? What would drive a child to kill the father and/or mother who love and care for him?*

Because I am a black man, I can understand some of the issues. For years I had repressed anger against white people in successful ministries. I felt that I wasn't given a fair chance at a successful ministry because I'm black, and I was angry with God and with successful white ministers. God began dealing with me in the area of anger that, in my case, led to resentment and bitterness. The Lord told me, "Mack, I want to bring you up to My standards. I don't want you to live in anger." Then He began to show me great leaders in the Bible who had good reasons to become angry, bitter and resentful. Yet they did not succumb to the temptation. They controlled their anger, and God gave them the victory.

I (Brenda) remember my father was an alcoholic when I was a child, and my brothers took responsibility for the family. When our mother passed away, they couldn't find my father, and their burden became greater. They were very angry and often said, "If we ever get hold of him, he's a dead man." But thank God, through prayer my family was saved. Within three years God brought my entire family to the East Coast to meet my father. He repented and asked for forgiveness for not being there when we needed him, and our family relationships were restored.

By sharing our experiences with you and looking into the Word of God, we believe this book will help you discover:

- God's description of various types of anger

- How to be angry without sinning
- The nature of anger as a gauge for maturity in your life
- The difference between "clamming up" and "blowing up"
- Pressure points to avoid
- Productive ways to channel anger
- Eight steps to overcome anger

God has given us the victory over anger, and He wants you to walk in victory! Because He is our heavenly Father, He desires to give us good things, discipline us in love and bless us. Our prayer is that the words of this book will speak hope, joy and peace in the Holy Ghost into your life.

ONE

ANGER: THE CONSTRUCTIVE AND DESTRUCTIVE EMOTION

Have you ever noticed how clever store managers place candy next to the checkout counter to entice children? Two-year-old Johnny sees all this candy and bubble gum and wants it all.

"Hey, my candy, mine!" he says, yelling and whining.

Mama replies, "You can't have that, Johnny."

"My candy. Mine!"

Johnny doesn't know that the candy is not free, so he takes some and tries to leave the store without paying for it. His mother takes the candy away and puts it back. The next thing you know the child is on the floor, throwing a temper tantrum — kicking, screaming and crying — like somebody is trying to kill him. He's angry because he can't have his way.

Finally the mother gives in to the child and says, "Go on and get it." She buys the candy and gives it to him, thinking it's going to pacify him, but all she's doing is increasing the child's desire to control. Little Johnny grows up using anger as a way to control situations and people.

Many adults start out just like Johnny. Once they reach adulthood, anger becomes a destructive force in their lives because nobody has shown them the proper way to handle it. Anger — like power, sex or fire — is not wrong, but it is important to know how to use it. Anger becomes carnal when we take the extreme of either blowing up or clamming up, which we will discuss later.

Who's in Control of Your House?

Our environment determines whether our minds are controlled by the Spirit or the carnal man. The carnal man will grow and take over if we allow our environment to foster his growth. If we do nothing, the carnal man automatically grows because living on earth creates an atmosphere for carnal growth. So we must encourage spiritual growth by controlling our environment.

Continuously feeding our spirit man with the Word of God is the only way we can control anger. James says, "Receive with meekness the implanted word, which is able to save your souls" (1:21).

Anger, if left uncontrolled, gives the devil a foothold (Eph. 4:26-27). The last thing we want to do is give place to the devil!

The first area the devil attacks is our minds. He begins by planting hurts into them — real or imagined. That's why Ephesians 4:23 says: "Be renewed in the spirit of your mind." The Greek word for *renewed* is *ananeoo*, which means "to be continually made young by the Spirit controlling your mind."[1]

Our minds have a spirit too! And we've got to decide which spirit — the carnal or the spiritual — we will allow to control our minds. We've got to put the Spirit of Christ into our minds. Philippians 2:5 says, "Let this mind be in you which was also in Christ Jesus."

When we give way to the carnal spirit, Satan gains entrance into our minds, our emotions and our wills. Our actions become no different than an unsaved individual. We give the devil access to our spirits as born-again Christians when we say by our actions, "Lord, I deny You, and I don't want to serve You anymore. You are not my Lord." God's Word tells us, "Therefore submit to God. Resist the devil and he will flee from you" (James 4:7). In other words, if we submit our lives, will and desires to God and allow Him to work in us, then we will desire to do His will because He has revealed it through His Word, and His Word is in us.

It's a choice we make. We choose either to obey God's Word or to do what pleases us. We live and work in the world — everything we do takes place in the natural world. But God has given us the Holy Spirit to help us control our emotions. We were created by God to be emotional beings, but not to be led by our emotions. Be led by the Spirit of God (Rom. 8:14).

Anger, like most emotions, can be either a constructive or a destructive force. A person who is angry about a situation may use that emotion as a motivation to change things. Candy Lightner, who started MADD (Mothers Against Drunk Driving), turned her anger into a constructive force. She got angry enough to do something when a drunk driver killed her thirteen-year-old daughter.[2]

As a result, MADD has become one of the most prominent traffic safety and victim assistance organizations. Since its founding in 1980, drunk driving has decreased by 40 percent. Also, more than two thousand anti-drunk driving laws have passed, and thousands of victims of drunk driving have been supported by MADD.[3] This is just one example of constructive anger.

In the Bible, we find an example of destructive anger. Moses, although he was a great man and a powerful leader, allowed his self-destructive anger to get him in trouble with God.

Then the Lord spoke to Moses, saying,

"Take the rod; you and your brother
Aaron gather the congregation together.
Speak to the rock before their eyes, and
it will yield its water; thus you shall bring
water for them out of the rock, and give
drink to the congregation and their animals" (Num. 20:7-8).

God told Moses to *speak* to the rock, but look at
what Moses decided to do.

And Moses and Aaron gathered the assembly together before the rock; and he said
to them, "Hear now, you rebels! Must we
bring water for you out of this rock?"
Then Moses lifted his hand and struck
the rock twice with his rod; and water
came out abundantly (Num. 20:10-11).

Moses was a little bit upset at the children of
Israel. Moses' uncontrolled anger impaired his
judgment and led him to disobey God's orders. As
a result, he was denied entrance into the Promised
Land.

Then the Lord spoke to Moses and
Aaron, "Because you did not believe Me,
to hallow Me in the eyes of the children
of Israel, therefore you shall not bring
this assembly into the land which I have
given them" (Num. 20:12).

Sometimes we miss out on God's promises
because we allow destructive anger to cloud our

minds and impair our judgment. When we don't obey God, we keep ourselves from walking in His promises. We become impatient and take matters into our own hands saying, "I'll take care of this situation myself. I can see I'm getting nowhere fast." It breaks God's heart when we lose faith in Him because we don't believe He's big enough to handle the situation.

Destructive anger keeps us from getting promoted in life. Learning how to handle anger is an essential key to receiving promotion and to doing great things for God. People who lose control over their emotions are people who usually spend a lot of time alone because they drive away the people around them. Just as people who are in high-volume sales know how to handle rejection, people who win in life know how to control their emotions.

WATCH YOUR TONGUE!

In Ephesians 4:26, the Greek word used for *anger* is *orgizo,* which means "to become exasperated."[4] Paul warns us about the dangers of destructive anger:

> "Be angry and do not sin": do not let the
> sun go down on your wrath (Eph. 4:26).

This verse talks about controlling anger before it takes root and moves us into sin. How does anger move us into sin? The first place anger takes root is in our mouths. One of the sharpest weapons of anger is the tongue.

Likewise the tongue is a small part of the body, but it makes great boasts Consider what a great forest is set on fire by a small spark. The tongue also is a fire, a world of evil among the parts of the body. It corrupts the whole person, sets the whole course of his life on fire, and is itself set on fire by hell (James 3:5-6, NIV).

The words that roll off our tongues reveal what is in our hearts. The Word of God tells us that "out of the abundance of the heart the mouth speaks" (Matt. 12:34). We can speak the truth about things that make us angry without losing our cool.

There are many verses in the Bible about God's anger. When our God-given rights are threatened or violated, it is possible to display good anger, as we'll see in the next chapter.

RIGHTEOUS INDIGNATION

How often have we heard someone piously declare that his anger is "righteous indignation"? Many people use this as an excuse for ungodly anger. The same things that arouse God's anger should arouse righteous indignation in us.

The Scriptures declare that God's nature is merciful, gracious, long-suffering and abounding in goodness and truth (Ex. 34:5-6). However, it is man's continuous sinful nature that can arouse God's anger. But not before He forewarns us and patiently instructs us through the Bible and by His messengers and teachers. God's anger is never without justification.

The Bible contains many references to anger, particularly God's anger. When referring to the Scriptures about God's anger, the key is to look at the context of each verse and determine how God's anger was justified. Below are twelve traits that provoke godly anger.

1. STUBBORNNESS

The number one trait that makes God angry is stubbornness. I (Mack) was stubborn when God called me to carry His Word and to pastor our church, Christian Faith Center, in the town of Creedmoor, North Carolina.

I remember praying out loud, "Lord, evidently You don't know what pastors go through. Everybody knows me as Mack Jr. I'll never be able to pastor. What am I going to tell the people?"

"The Bible," He said.

"But my first-grade teacher goes to that church. Even the school janitor goes there! What can I tell the people?"

Again He responded, "The Bible." I'm so glad I obeyed His voice. I delight in serving God and His people.

In Exodus 32 God's wrath was kindled against the Israelites because they were "a stiffnecked people."

And the Lord said to Moses, "I have seen this people, and indeed it is a stiff-necked people! Now therefore, let Me alone, that My wrath may burn hot against them and I may consume them (vv. 9-10).

God didn't need to tell Moses He was angry with the people. But God forewarned Moses so that he would intercede on their behalf and the Israelites would humble themselves before God (v. 11). God could have wiped them all out, but it was as if God said, "Moses, hold Me back."

But they did not listen or pay attention; instead, they followed the stubborn inclinations of their evil hearts. They went backward and not forward (Jer. 7:24, NIV).

The Israelites' stubbornness blinded them from seeing God's original plan. Although they disobeyed God, He fulfilled His promise to them. But it took them longer than a few days to reach the Promised Land. It took forty years to be exact.

Stubbornness will be a setback in every area of our lives. When we refuse to obey God we are blinded by self-ambition. Although God in His mercy will fulfill His promises to us, it will take us twice as long to reach the goal if we follow our own plans.

2. Idolatry

Some people spend more time worshiping a

boat or a car than worshiping God. There's nothing wrong with having material things, but our worship time with God is more important. For example, if you want to go boating on Sunday occasionally, that's OK. But be sure to attend a worship service another day of the week. Family, friends, a job, money — and even church activities — can become idols without our realizing it. A person can even idolize himself, which the Bible calls arrogance.

> For rebellion is like the sin of divination, and *arrogance* like the evil of idolatry. Because you have rejected the word of the Lord, he has rejected you as king (1 Sam. 15:23, NIV, italics added).

The Lord rejected Saul because he thought he had arrived — he thought he was the man of the hour. But God said, "Not so, Saul. You have rebelled against Me, and you are so prideful that you consider yourself to be above My word."

God compares arrogance to idolatry because anyone who idolizes his thoughts, ideas, opinions and words above God's dethrones Jesus from His rightful place in the person's heart. Arrogance says, "I believe I am god. I am in charge of my destiny."

> In his pride the wicked does not seek him; in all his thoughts there is no room for God (Ps. 10:4, NIV).

We were created by God to worship Him with our whole hearts, knowing that His ways and thoughts are higher than our own (Is. 55:8-9). As our Father, God always has our best interests at heart.

3. MURMURING

Have you ever heard someone murmur, "Lord, why can't I have this or that?" or have you ever prayed like that?

I (Mack) used to murmur, "Dear God, why are You sending me to Creedmoor? Why can't You send me to Durham or Raleigh where there are some stoplights?"

Everyone at one time or another has murmured in their hearts about the little things they're asked to do on the job, at home or at church. People say things such as: "If I just had a better job and made more money, I would be happy"; "I would be happier if I were married and/or if I had children"; "Why does my wife have to nag me to mow the lawn?"; "How come the pastor never asks me to head up a committee? How come he always asks Sister So-and-so instead?"; or "Is this rain ever going to let up? When will we see some sunshine?"

When we murmur, we become self-centered instead of Christ-centered. We focus on the people and circumstances in our lives instead of Christ. If ever there were whiners and complainers, they were the children of Israel (Num. 11:1). They experienced deliverance and witnessed awesome

21

miracles at the hand of God, and they still complained. They longed for Egypt and what it could give them (even though God's resources were limitless and Egypt's were limited).

> Now the mixed multitude who were among them yielded to intense craving; so the children of Israel also wept again and said: "Who will give us meat to eat? We remember the fish which we ate freely in Egypt, the cucumbers, the melons, the leeks, the onions, and the garlic; but now our whole being is dried up; there is nothing at all except this manna before our eyes!"
>
> So the Lord said to Moses..."Then you shall say to the people...'Therefore the Lord will give you meat, and you shall eat. You shall eat, not one day, nor two days, nor five days, nor ten days, nor twenty days, but for a whole month, until it comes out of your nostrils and becomes loathsome to you, because you have despised the Lord who is among you, and have wept before Him, saying, "Why did we ever come up out of Egypt?"'
>
> Now a wind went out from the Lord, and it brought quail from the camp...And the people stayed up all that day, all night, and all the next day, and gathered the quail...and they spread them out for themselves all around the camp. But while the meat was still between their teeth, before

it was chewed, the wrath of the Lord was aroused against the people, and the Lord struck the people with a very great plague (Num. 11:4-6,16a,18-20,31-33).

The Bible tells us that although God sent fresh, just-add-water instant manna every day, the Israelites still complained because they didn't have meat. So God sent them meat, but they continued to murmur against God and provoked His wrath. God's holy character can't tolerate sin. God's wrath isn't irrational and fitful like human anger. It is in no way vindictive or malicious. Unlike human anger, God's wrath is an expression of His holy love.[1]

Paul said concerning the former conversation — the former lifestyle, the former way of behavior — to put off the old man (Eph. 4:22). The old man grows increasingly corrupt through deceitful lusts and does not have the Spirit of God in him. Deceitful lusting is more than physically lusting after another person. We can lust after a former lifestyle, power, money, position and so on.

Deceitful lust sends out a message that if the desire is fulfilled, lust will be satisfied. But when we do give in to it, lust says, "I am not satisfied. I want more." It's deceitful because it doesn't bring joy. It may bring pleasure but only for a season (Eccl. 2:1-3). When that season is over, death will follow, as it did for the Israelites. Their lustful, selfish desires for Egypt caused them to murmur against God and His provision for them.

We don't impress God by murmuring. Whatever your vocation in life, whatever God asks of you, do it wholeheartedly, as serving the Lord and not men, knowing that He will reward you (Eph. 6:7-8).

4. PRIDE

Some men feel that breaking down and crying is a sign of weakness. It takes a humble man to acknowledge that he's hurting and needs God's help. The truth is that most women appreciate men who are vulnerable in front of others. But pride may hinder men from receiving deliverance if they know women are present.

For this reason, we sometimes hold separate meetings for men and women during our conferences. During one of these conferences we dealt with men who were angry with their fathers. Some of them didn't know who their fathers were or where to find them. Their fathers were never there for them during their childhood. We had these men come to the altar, repent and release their emotions. Many of them wept bitterly and cried out loud. A man normally doesn't cry in front of others unless pride has been removed from his life.

Pride tends to blind us to our own weakness. Pride majors in selfish reasoning instead of seeking God's purpose in a matter.

A man's pride will bring him low, but the humble in spirit will retain honor (Prov. 29:23).

5. SELF-WILL

Self-will says, "I don't need God or anybody else. I can do it my*self.*" Self-will causes us to do things on impulse instead of waiting on God for the answer. It closes the door of opportunity to receive God's blessings. Simeon's and Levi's self-wills prevented them from inheriting the land that was promised to them.

> For in their anger they slew a man, and in their self-will they hamstrung an ox. Cursed be their anger, for it is fierce; and their wrath, for it is cruel! I will divide them in Jacob and scatter them in Israel (Gen. 49:6-7).

Many times we don't realize that by being self-willed, we are in essence telling God we don't need or want His help. When we try to do things in our strength, we get ourselves into a dilemma and then blame God for the outcome. We get angry with God when He doesn't respond to our selfish prayers. Self-will leads to self-destruction. God longs to bless His children, but He will not pour out His blessings if He sees a self-willed attitude within us. God looks for a humble and contrite heart (Ps. 51:17).

6. ADULTERY

God ordained sex to unite a husband and wife spiritually as well as physically. Adultery makes Him angry because it violates the marriage covenant. God knows the various repercussions of this sin: shame, guilt, emotional pain inflicted on other family members, an unwanted pregnancy and so on.

> Do you not know that your bodies are members of Christ? Shall I then take the members of Christ and make them members of a harlot? Certainly not! Or do you not know that he who is joined to a harlot is one body with her? For "the two," He says, "shall become one flesh..." Or do you not know that your body is the temple of the Holy Spirit who is in you, whom you have from God, and you are not your own? For you were bought at a price; therefore glorify God in your body and in your spirit, which are God's (1 Cor. 6:15-16,19-20).

Why does it seem that God judges adultery on a different scale? Because the sexual relationship is the only act given to man by God that creates a human life — an eternal soul.

7. REBELLION

Moses sent out a spy from each of the twelve tribes of Israel to explore Canaan. But Joshua and Caleb were the only ones who came back with a positive outlook. The others saw the giants in the land and began to murmur, causing the people to rebel. Both Joshua and Caleb pleaded with the people to move by faith and claim the Promised Land.

> Then Caleb quieted the people before Moses, and said, "Let us go up at once and take possession, for we are well able to overcome it." But the men who had gone up with him said, "We are not able to go up against the people, for they are stronger than we...There we saw the giants (the descendants of Anak came from the giants); and we were like grasshoppers in our own sight, and so we were in their sight" (Num. 13:30-31,33).

Joshua and Caleb continued to admonish the people of Israel to move into obedience instead of rebellion against God. The people looked at the obstacle instead of God's power to deliver them.

> The land we passed through to spy out is an exceedingly good land. If the Lord delights in us, then He will bring us into this land and give it to us, "a land which flows with milk and honey." Only do not rebel against the Lord, nor fear the people of the land (Num. 14:7-9).

Notice in verse 9 that the words *rebel* and *fear* are in the same sentence. When we allow fear to paralyze us and prevent us from achieving God's vision, we also find ourselves rebelling against God. God's vision for our lives is always much larger than what we can accomplish in our own abilities and talents so that He gets all the glory. He requires faith through obedience to accomplish His purposes for our lives.

8. BACKSLIDING

> I will heal their backsliding, I will love them freely, for My anger has turned away from him (Hos. 14:4).

After experiencing many victories, the Israelites turned their backs on God in pursuit of other gods. Although the action of backsliding angered God, He never stopped loving His bride — Israel. He wooed her back to Himself with an everlasting love.

There are times in our lives when God allows certain situations and circumstances to occur to remind us of our need for Him. It is during these seasons of testing that we must avoid listening to the voices of fear and doubt that will move us into backsliding.

Even in the midst of fear and turmoil, we are urged to put into remembrance what God said by holding fast to it and confessing it. We can focus on the mind of God through fasting and prayer, and that will protect us from backsliding. Fear keeps us focused on self while prayer keeps us focused on God.

9. UNREPENTANCE

Because our lives affect many others for good or evil, God's wrath will move against those who purposefully rebel against Him and the truth by their unrighteous lifestyles.

> For the wrath of God is revealed from heaven against all ungodliness and unrighteousness of men, who suppress the truth in unrighteousness (Rom. 1:18).

God's anger is kindled when the heart is not repentant of unrighteousness. God becomes an enemy to those who rebel against Him. Sin chokes out the light and gives way to the darkness in our hearts. By choosing to ignore the still, small voice of the Lord and willfully disobeying Him, we give sin dominion over us.

10. DISOBEDIENCE

Uzzah and David learned a hard lesson — you don't mess with God. The ark represented the holy presence of God, and God gave specific instructions that it was to be carried by hand (Num. 7:4-9). David and his associates knew it was wrong to put the ark on a cart, but they stubbornly defied God's commandment.

> And David arose and went with all the people who were with him from Baale Judah to bring up from there the ark of God, whose name is called by the Name,

29

the Lord of Hosts. So they set the ark of God on a new cart, and brought it out of the house of Abinadab, which was on the hill; and Uzzah and Ahio, the sons of Abinadab, drove the new cart. And they brought it out of the house of Abinadab, which was on the hill, accompanying the ark of God; and Ahio went before the ark...And when they came to Nachon's threshing floor, Uzzah put out his hand to the ark of God and took hold of it, for the oxen stumbled. Then the anger of the Lord was aroused against Uzzah, and God struck him there for his error; and he died there by the ark of God. And David became angry because of the Lord's outbreak against Uzzah; and he called the name of the place Perez Uzzah to this day (2 Sam. 6:2-4,6-8).

Although Uzzah's intentions were good, it was the irreverence for God's instructions and presence that led to Uzzah's death. He became an example to David and all of Israel that the presence of God is not to be taken lightly. He is a holy God, and He is to be feared.

11. SPIRITUALISM

God desires for His people to follow the teachings and instructions of His prophets, not of psychics. God's warning concerning the following of a spiritist, or medium, was specific.

> When you come into the land which the Lord your God is giving you, you shall not learn to follow the abominations of those nations. There shall not be found among you anyone who makes his son or his daughter pass through the fire, or one who practices witchcraft, or a soothsayer, or one who interprets omens, or a sorcerer, or one who conjures spells, or a medium, or a spiritist, or one who calls up the dead. For all who do these things are an abomination to the Lord, and because of these abominations the Lord your God drives them out from before you (Deut. 18:9-12).

King Saul disobeyed the commandment of God and sought a medium instead of God concerning his future and the future of Israel. This sin angered God and cost the life of Saul and his sons in a war against the Philistines (1 Sam. 28:11-19).

God created us with a need for fellowship with Him and man. When we have fellowship and communion with God, He instructs us in the ways of life.

In Romans 8:2, Paul writes regarding two kinds of laws — the law of sin and death and the law of the Spirit of life in Christ Jesus. Fellowship and communion with spiritualism involve cooperating with the demonic realm of influence. From the days of Moses, God has commanded that we have no other gods before Him.

God has placed and ordained ministry gifts such

as the apostle, prophet, evangelist, pastor and teacher for the perfecting and maturing of His church. Through these ministry gifts we are to receive instructions and guidance concerning our lives in spiritual and practical matters. God's anger arises toward us if we seek counsel or guidance from any sources other than those that He has ordained or set in the church (Eph. 4:11-12).

12. WICKEDNESS

The Bible teaches a balanced perspective about God's nature. Although He is loving, long-suffering, merciful and kind, He is also just. His anger is kindled when workers of iniquity have unrepentant hearts. For example, in Exodus 34:6-7, God makes a strong declaration to those who practice wickedness.

> And the Lord passed by before him, and proclaimed, "The Lord, the Lord God, merciful and gracious, longsuffering, and abounding in goodness and truth, keeping mercy for thousands, forgiving iniquity and transgression and sin, by no means clearing the guilty, visiting the iniquity of the fathers upon the children and the children's children to the third and the fourth generation."

He started this portion of Scripture with a promise to extend mercy to thousands who repent. Yet, God doesn't dismiss the unrepentant. The destruction of the whole earth by a flood in Noah's day, the destruction of Sodom and Gomorrah, and the forsaking of the nation of Israel for four hundred years in Egypt are all examples that God has standards for us to follow. There are painful consequences to disobedience when we refuse to walk and live according to His standards.

As we will see in the next chapter, Jesus displayed anger just as His Father did. But His anger was against sinful attitudes and actions. Thank God that through Jesus' blood, today we can experience God's grace and not His wrath. He is the God of a second chance.

THREE

UNDER THE LAW
OF GRACE

Have you ever felt God was angry with you and was punishing you? How many times have you heard the phrase, "God hates the sin, but He loves the sinner" (see Heb. 12:5-6)? God's anger as displayed in the Old Testament was directed at sin, not at people. God is a just God who measures every situation by the standard of righteousness.

Our actions and attitude of heart determine God's reaction toward us. There are some that He deals with harsher than others as we will see later. Because of His love and long-suffering toward us, God's anger is not easily aroused. It is continuous rebellion and sin that arouse His anger. "God is a just judge, and God is angry with the wicked every day" (Ps. 7:11).

A CHANCE TO REPENT

When God does become angry with sin, He confronts sinners in order to give them a chance to repent. Jesus gave various examples of how to confront someone. There were times when He confronted people with only a few words. Look at the example of the woman caught in adultery.

> Then the scribes and Pharisees brought to Him a woman caught in adultery. And when they had set her in the midst, they said to Him, "Teacher, this woman was caught in adultery, in the very act. Now Moses, in the law, commanded us that such should be stoned. But what do You say?" This they said, testing Him, that they might have something of which to accuse Him. But Jesus stooped down and wrote on the ground with His finger, as though He did not hear. So when they continued asking Him, He raised Himself up and said to them, "He who is without sin among you, let him throw a stone at her first."

And again He stooped down and wrote
on the ground. Then those who heard it,
being convicted by their conscience,
went out one by one, beginning with the
oldest even to the last. And Jesus was left
alone, and the woman standing in the
midst. When Jesus had raised Himself up
and saw no one but the woman, He said
to her, "Woman, where are those accusers
of yours? Has no one condemned you?"
She said, "No one, Lord." And Jesus said
to her, "Neither do I condemn you; go
and sin no more" (John 8:3-11).

Jesus confronted both the Pharisees and the
woman but in two different ways. He confronted
the woman's accusers by showing that everyone
has sinned. Hypocritically, they had pointed out
her sin while ignoring their own. No one is without
sin. But God's grace and mercy abound so that
those who do sin might repent and be saved. Yet
Jesus didn't let the woman off the hook. He confronted her with her sin, but He did it gently without
condemning her. The Lord's gentle approach helped
her to accept salvation.

Sometimes in our attempts to correct a matter,
we as Christians become so judgmental that we
forget to display God's love and mercy. We must
have the mind of Christ in every situation.
Otherwise, we can easily slip into sin by having a
self-righteous attitude and thus ruin our witness to
others.

A CHANCE FOR SPIRITUAL RESTORATION

Jesus used confrontation to help people see the condition of their souls. Take, for example, the Samaritan woman at the well. Jesus approached the woman by asking her for a drink of water. Samaritans were part of a mixed race and were only half-Jewish. Her reply to Jesus showed her surprise that a Jewish man, of all people, would acknowledge her, much less speak to her.

> Jesus answered and said to her, "Whoever drinks of this water will thirst again, but whoever drinks of the water that I shall give him will never thirst. But the water that I shall give him will become in him a fountain of water springing up into ever-lasting life." The woman said to Him, "Sir, give me this water, that I may not thirst, nor come here to draw." Jesus said to her, "Go, call your husband, and come here." The woman answered and said, "I have no husband." Jesus said to her, "You have well said, 'I have no husband,' for you have had five husbands, and the one whom you now have is not your husband; in that you spoke truly" (John 4:13-18).

Jesus knew the woman was living in sin, but instead of rejecting her, He used confrontation to help her see her spiritual condition. Again, He confronted the sin in the person's life without placing the individual under condemnation. It has never been God's plan to bring us under condemnation when confronting our spiritual condition; it is His plan to reconcile us to Him.

> Brethren, if a man is overtaken in any trespass, you who are spiritual restore such a one in a spirit of gentleness, considering yourself lest you also be tempted. Bear one another's burdens, and so fulfill the law of Christ (Gal. 6:1-2).

THE LAW OF LOVE VERSUS THE LAW OF LEGALISM

Jesus also confronted those ignorant of the law by patiently explaining it to them. He had a soft heart toward those who innocently sought the truth.

> But when the Pharisees heard that He had silenced the Sadducees, they gathered together. Then one of them, a lawyer, asked Him a question, testing Him, and saying, "Teacher, which is the great commandment in the law?" Jesus said to him, "'You shall love the Lord your God with all your heart, with all your soul, and with all your mind.' This is the first and great commandment. And the second is like it: 'You shall love your neighbor as yourself.' On these two commandments hang all the Law and the Prophets" (Matt. 22:34-40).

The Sadducees and the Pharisees sought to legalistically fulfill the law of Moses, but Jesus came to fulfill the law of love. Jesus declared these two commandments to be the greatest because God is love. We need to realize that there are those who are ignorant of the gospel and who don't have a saving knowledge of the person of Jesus Christ. We must display patience, love and tenderness toward these individuals when confronting them about any wrongdoing.

Jesus confronted the scribes and Pharisees — the church folk — many times. Jesus used harsh language to reprimand them. They knew the law (or at least claimed to), and yet they didn't practice what they preached (Matt. 23:3).

> And He entered the synagogue again, and a man was there who had a withered hand. So they watched Him closely, whether He would heal him on the Sabbath, so that they might accuse Him. And He said to the man who had the withered hand, "Step forward." Then He said to them, "Is it lawful on the Sabbath to do good or to do evil, to save life or to kill?" But they kept silent. And when He had looked around at them with anger, being grieved by the hardness of their hearts, He said to the man, "Stretch out your hand." And he stretched it out, and his hand was restored as whole as the other (Mark 3:1-5).

Earlier, Jesus rebuked the Pharisees by telling

them that the Sabbath was made for man, not man for the Sabbath (Mark 2:27). His anger was directed toward their attitudes and actions.

It was the leaders' hardness of heart that made Jesus angry. They placed the law above the needs of the people. Jesus said that hardness of heart was the main cause of divorce (Mark 10:4-6). (God hates the hardness of heart that causes divorce, but He loves the divorcee.)

Dishonesty and unfairness also made Jesus angry.

> So they came to Jerusalem. Then Jesus went into the temple and began to drive out those who bought and sold in the temple, and overturned the tables of the money changers and the seats of those who sold doves. And He would not allow anyone to carry wares through the temple. Then He taught, saying to them, "Is it not written, 'My house shall be called a house of prayer for all nations'? But you have made it a 'den of thieves'" (Mark 11:15-17).

Jesus said the money changers made His house a den of thieves. In other words, the money changers were robbing money from the people by not charging a fair market price. Jesus knew the high priests who owned the booths were charging unreasonable prices for sacrificial animals and that the exchange rates were highway robbery. Jesus wasn't angry about business transactions taking place. Jesus was angry about the dishonesty and unfairness toward the people.

When we first started to sell tapes years ago, some churches we visited said, "No, you can't sell those tapes in here." Then they would quickly point out the scripture in Mark 11:17 and interpret it to mean that nothing could be sold in God's house. But Mark 11:17 didn't apply to our tape sales because we didn't sell the tapes during the service. We charged a fair price for our products, too. We still do. We're not stealing from God's people by the prices we charge. Although we have a different interpretation for this scripture, we abided by their wishes.

Some people rent property to others and charge ridiculous amounts. A landlord should give his tenants a fair deal or else he'll get in trouble with God for overcharging.

Let's look at another thing that made Jesus angry — hypocrisy. Jesus was not intimidated by the scribes and the Pharisees. Forget the picture of Jesus portrayed in Sunday school; Jesus was not a wimp. He was physically strong and spoke with authority. Jesus compared the scribes and Pharisees to whitewashed sepulchres because they looked clean on the outside, but inside they were dead.

> Woe to you, scribes and Pharisees, hypocrites! For you pay tithe of mint and anise and cummin, and have neglected the weightier matters of the law: justice and mercy and faith. These you ought to have done, without leaving the others undone...Woe to you, scribes and Pharisees, hypocrites! For you cleanse

the outside of the cup and dish, but inside they are full of extortion and self-indulgence. Blind Pharisee, first cleanse the inside of the cup and dish, that the outside of them may be clean also...For you are like whitewashed tombs which indeed appear beautiful outwardly, but inside are full of dead men's bones and all uncleanness. Even so you also outwardly appear righteous to men, but inside you are full of hypocrisy and lawlessness (Matt. 23:23,25-28).

Outwardly everything looked good, but spiritually speaking, they were full of dead men's bones and all uncleanliness. Jesus boldly addressed the church leaders, and He wasn't biting His tongue about speaking the truth. He was telling them, "You're so worried about the little things that you're ignoring what really counts — justice, mercy and faith!"

When we place more emphasis on outward appearance than on our relationship with God, we become spiritually controlling. We've been in churches where they jumped on Brenda because of her outward appearance. They didn't like the earrings and the makeup.

It's not wrong to dress well, but there needs to be a balance. We need to take care of our outward appearance without allowing it to become more important than our spiritual condition. God's Word calls us hypocrites if we emphasize the outward appearance and neglect the condition of our hearts.

Once we went to a church and Mack placed his Bible on the communion table. The members were angry because to them nothing should go on the communion table. They made the wood table an idol.

When we're blind to our own faults, we become critical of others and worship things associated with the person of Jesus Christ more than Jesus Christ Himself. We go to church and get involved in ministries to drown out the Spirit's voice which convicts us of our own sins. Doing good works, tithing and attending church weekly are not worship. These actions are merely tradition if we don't do them out of our love for God.

> Then the scribes and Pharisees who were from Jerusalem came to Jesus, saying "Why do Your disciples transgress the tradition of the elders? For they do not wash their hands when they eat bread." He answered and said to them, "Why do you also transgress the commandment of God because of your tradition?...'These people draw near to Me with their mouth, and honor Me with their lips, but their heart is far from Me. And in vain they worship Me, teaching as doctrines the commandments of men...' Hear and understand: Not what goes into the mouth defiles a man; but what comes out of the mouth, this defiles a man" (Matt. 15:1-3,8-11).

The scribes' and Pharisees' hearts were far from

God. He was angry with them because their worship was nothing more than lip service. Jesus confronted and offended the leaders because He and the disciples didn't follow their traditional religious rules. Likewise, when we place more emphasis on church rituals and the law than on becoming Christ-like and loving God, we miss the true meaning of Christianity.

> For sin shall not be your master, because you are not under law, but under grace. What then? Shall we sin because we are not under law but under grace? By no means! (Rom. 6:14-15, NIV).

In other words, Paul was saying that even though we sin, we are no longer bound to the law. The law in its entirety as the Pharisees knew it was given by one man, Moses. And by one man, Jesus Christ, the law of sin was eliminated so that men are no longer slaves to it. We have been set free to receive God's grace and forgiveness. However, we can't become careless with our spiritual lives. We must guard ourselves from allowing anger to move us into sin. As we said earlier, we are surrounded by a carnal environment, but we are controlled by the Spirit.

> For the sinful nature desires what is contrary to the Spirit, and the Spirit what is contrary to the sinful nature. They are in conflict with each other, so that you do not do what you want. But if you are led

by the Spirit, you are not under law. The acts of the sinful nature are obvious: sexual immorality, impurity and debauchery; idolatry and witchcraft; *hatred, discord, jealousy, fits of rage,* selfish ambition, dissensions, factions and envy; drunkenness, orgies, and the like. I warn you, as I did before, that those who live like this will not inherit the kingdom of God (Gal. 5:17-21, NIV, italics added).

Notice fits of rage in that bunch? It's no coincidence that hatred, discord and jealousy are tied to anger. These demonic influences hang out together, and when we submit to them they result in fits of rage.

When we speak against things that ignite God's anger, we need to be sure that we are speaking in love and that the fruits of the Spirit are evident in our lives (Gal. 5:22-23). Speaking in the name of honesty or righteous indignation becomes dangerous if we're not careful how we vocalize our anger. It can cause chaos and ruin our testimony.

In the next chapter we will learn to vent anger and release the pressure so it doesn't cause destruction. If done the right way, expressing anger can bring forgiveness and healing.

Four

Letting Off Steam
Without Getting Burnt

People with repressed anger are like pressure cookers. If a pressure cooker doesn't have an out-let to let off steam, it eventually explodes, and the food that was inside ends up all over the place. You have to let the cooker cool down, run it under cool water and then gently release the pressure.

In the same way, repressed anger causes a person

to explode, making a mess of things. Brenda says that when she gets angry, she can feel her nose spread. But when I (Mack) repress anger, I feel a tightness inside. This pent-up energy turns into bitterness. In Hebrews 12 Paul warns us against allowing bitterness to take root in our lives.

> Pursue peace with all people, and holiness, without which no one will see the Lord: looking carefully lest anyone fall short of the grace of God; lest any root of bitterness springing up cause trouble, and by this many become defiled (Heb. 12:14-15).

Allowing bitterness into our lives is destructive to others as well as to ourselves. In verse 15, the Greek word for *bitterness* is *pikria* which means "acridity (especially poison)."[1] It's a bitterness so strong that it poisons your system — body and soul.

Similarly, when the nervous system is overstimulated it produces toxic amounts of stomach acid that cause ulcers. The first thing a doctor usually asks a patient with ulcers is what kind of work he does. Then he tries to find out if the patient is under a lot of stress. Although the patient appears calm on the outside, inside his body may be reacting to a stressful situation.

For the most part, I (Mack) have been blessed with good health. But I have had a few times when I could trace an illness back to anger over a situation or against a person.

Some time ago, I walked around for months with excruciating back pain. I had repressed anger toward people who had hurt me regarding my role as pastor. I also was carrying anger in my spirit against a minister who told another minister something about me that simply was not true. In an attempt to vindicate myself by scheduling a meeting with the men, I suddenly became physically ill. The stress of anticipating the meeting to express my side of the story produced enough pain to land me in bed for a couple of days. As I was praying about my healing, the Holy Spirit asked me to release the whole situation to Him. I cancelled the meeting, and I have not rescheduled it to this day. I learned a vital lesson: Release people and your anger toward them in order to have good health.

IRRECONCILABLE DIFFERENCES

In the same way that bitterness is a poison to our system, bitter words acts like a poison to others. James warns us that the tongue contains a deadly poison.

> All kinds of animals, birds, reptiles and creatures of the sea are being tamed and have been tamed by man, but no man can tame the tongue. It is a restless evil, full of deadly poison (James 3:7-8, NIV).

Most women want to confront those who offend them and discuss situations that bother them. When

I (Brenda) get angry with someone, I approach him and say, "What you did rubbed me the wrong way. I feel I need to let you know so we can reconcile our relationship." Once we discuss it, I release my anger, and I forgive him as well as ask for his forgiveness.

> And do not grieve the Holy Spirit of God, by whom you were sealed for the day of redemption. Let all bitterness, wrath, anger, clamor, and evil speaking be put away from you, with all malice. And be kind to one another, tenderhearted, forgiving one another, even as God in Christ forgave you (Eph. 4:30-32).

When we forgive others and release anger, then happiness acts like a medicine (Prov. 17:22). Happiness goes straight to the heart and heals the resentment. It's a healing process. But if we stay angry, we grieve the Holy Spirit because we've allowed the carnal man to take control.

Remember, the devil uses people he knows make us angry. He's going to send them around all the time. The angrier we become, the more destruction we cause.

When we approach someone to reconcile a broken relationship, we need to watch what we say and do. David wrote in Psalm 19:14:

> Let the words of my mouth and the meditation of my heart, be acceptable in Your sight, O Lord, my strength and my Redeemer.

49

The first thing off the top of our heads shouldn't be the first thing to come out of our mouths.

> My dear brothers, take note of this: Everyone should be quick to listen, slow to speak and slow to become angry, for man's anger does not bring about the righteous life that God desires (James 1:19-20, NIV).

God gave us two ears and one mouth so we can listen twice as much as we talk. Reaching the boiling point doesn't give us the right to let anger spill over and burn the other person. Angry words only lead to more trouble. When we exercise self-control over anger or any other emotion, we are wiser and stronger than the greatest conqueror (Prov. 16:32).

Perhaps you're thinking, *OK. I want to forgive the other person, but I don't know how to forgive or where to begin.* Below are four steps to forgiveness:

1. GIVE VALUE TO PEOPLE.

Don't belittle people by name-calling. When we use derogatory names or comments, we are only trying to justify our hatred toward them. Instead, seek to see the person as someone God created in His image. Each person has worth in God's eyes.

Purpose in your heart to be sensitive to the other person's needs instead of becoming so preoccupied with your own interests. What situation and circumstances is he facing? What interests him, and how can you best serve him? It's important to spend time with people in order to build healthy, rewarding relationships.

2. RELEASE THE HURTS — PAST AND PRESENT — TO GOD.

Unforgiveness is simply our way of justifying our hurt feelings and seeking revenge against the one who hurt us.

> And whenever you stand praying, if you have anything against anyone, forgive him, that your Father in heaven may also forgive you your trespasses (Mark 11:25).

By confessing our hurts to God, we surrender them to His care, and we surrender our rights to hold on to them. We must forgive and forget. A person may say, "Well, I forgive, but I won't ever forget!" Then he hasn't learned the real meaning of forgiveness.

When we keep a record of wrongs, we're not demonstrating agape love (1 Cor. 13:6). It's similar to running over a weed with the lawn mower. The weed disappears temporarily, but it will appear again and be stronger than ever. When we don't uproot our ill feelings by forgiving and forgetting, they will crop up later and be stronger than before.

3. PRAY FOR THE INDIVIDUAL(S) WHO HURT YOU.

We need to pray that our understanding would be opened to know that God's motivation is not to hurt but to heal. Jesus commanded us to pray for those who spitefully use us (Matt. 5:44). Jesus prayed in this fashion for those who crucified Him.

Father, forgive them, for they know not
what they do (Luke 23:34).

Offenses can affect us only as long as we allow
them to have power over us. Through prayer we
can release both the individual and the hurt.

4. BLESS HIM; DON'T CURSE HIM.

The law of sowing and reaping applies here.
When we bless someone — even if he or she curses
us — blessings will come back to us multiplied.

Rest in the Lord, and wait patiently for Him;
Do not fret because of him who prospers in
  his way,
Because of the man who brings wicked
  schemes to pass.
Cease from anger, and forsake wrath;
Do not fret — it only causes harm (Ps. 37:7-8).

Resting in the Lord means ceasing from your
own labors. In other words, allow God to handle
the situation. To *fret* implies "to eat or gnaw into."
When you see someone who seems to "get away
with murder," don't allow the injustice of it all to
gnaw at you. God has called you to forgive and to
put your feelings of anger to rest. If you allow the
spirit of forgiveness to operate in your life, you
will avoid two pitfalls of anger — blowing up and
clamming up.

DO YOU BLOW UP
OR CLAM UP?

Someone once said, "People who fly into a rage always make a bad landing." People who don't know how to channel their anger properly either fly off the handle or repress their anger to the point of becoming destructive. If you have a problem dealing with anger, chances are you do one of two things: Either you blow up or you clam up.

DON'T BLOW UP; GROW UP!

Blow-up anger is holding things inside that bother us without expressing our feelings. Blow-up anger usually results in some form of physical or verbal abuse such as actual physical attack, door slamming, reckless driving, put-downs, name-calling, yelling, temper outbursts, threats or sarcasm. Blowing up takes vengeance into our own hands. It's like trying to blow up a balloon until — boom! — it pops. The pressure in the balloon becomes more than it can contain.

For instance, an unsaved husband gets angry with his Christian wife because he feels she's attending church too much. She's not taking care of her household duties, much less him.

"Have you been back to church again?" he accuses.

"Yes, I've been back. Why?"

"You might try cleaning the house sometime before you go running off to church again."

"The Bible says to put God first. Don't jump on me about that now."

"But doesn't it also say that God is next to cleanliness. And you sure ain't clean!"

"You better watch it now. Look at my face. You better watch it now, 'cause you're making me angry."

"You better shut up, woman!"

"I thank God I have Jesus in me, because I would have clawed you."

Although both the wife and husband blew up in anger at each other, she finally subdued her anger.

In this situation she didn't show her husband a Christ-like attitude. But if she's led by the Spirit, the next time an argument arises, she'll trust God to take care of the situation.

Anger changes our facial expressions. Sometimes we see the spirit of anger operating in people. The angry person might not admit he's given into it, even though the veins in his neck start to swell.

If we don't soak our lives in God's Word on a daily basis, we will blow up. When we do explode, our immediate reaction is to retaliate against someone in the same way he hurt us. But the Word of God teaches us not to take vengeance into our hands. God will deal with those that hurt us.

> Do not repay anyone evil for evil. Be careful to do what is right in the eyes of everybody. If it is possible, as far as it depends on you, live at peace with everyone. Do not take revenge, my friends, but leave room for God's wrath, for it is written: "It is mine to avenge; I will repay," says the Lord (Rom. 12:17-19, NIV).

AN EMPTY WAGON MAKES A LOT OF NOISE

Clam-up anger is not expressing our angry feelings but instead continuing to hold a grudge. Clam-up anger is similar to a shaken soda can. From the outside you can't see the pressure built up inside the can. But when you open it, the pressure causes the soda to spray all over the place.

Many times we repress our true feelings and thoughts for fear that they will destroy a relationship or that we will lose control of a situation.

Clam-up anger affects our physical and emotional health, not to mention what it does to our spiritual lives! It can lead to physical problems such as obesity, insomnia, fatigue, backaches, headaches, skin conditions, gastrointestinal symptoms, ulcers and sexual problems. Some studies indicate that patients with chronic pain syndrome also show increased levels of anger.[1] Other studies say hostility is a leading factor in high blood pressure and heart problems.

We've all heard over the years the talk about "Type A" people. Type A people usually display certain characteristics. They talk fast; anticipate what's going to be said next; crave power and recognition; are compulsive about finishing things; tend to be easily aroused to anger by other people and things; and believe they can overcome anything if they try hard enough.[2]

Studies have shown that Type A personalities who smoke are more likely to increase their smoking habits than their Type B counterparts.[3] We've spoken to men who used to become angry when their families would hide the cigarettes from them so they would quit smoking. In their anger, these men would start arguments with family members.

People who clam up have certain personality traits. You may know someone with these traits or you may recognize them within yourself. Relatives or acquaintances of serial killers often say, "He never talked to anyone and was a hermit. I never would have thought he would do something like that."

An empty wagon makes a lot of noise. In other words, most people who talk a lot are not really dangerous. You need to watch out for the ones who hardly ever say anything. They can be the most destructive types. Often these people are:

- Quiet and soft-spoken.

- Willing to take the blame for anything just to keep the peace (even if it means never discussing the situation).

- The ones who take the absolute silent approach and deny that anything is wrong. They don't know what is upsetting them.

- Critical and sometimes sarcastic about everything. Their criticisms are often intellectual, rational criticisms with an undertone of anger, hostility and negativism.

How often do we read in the newspaper about someone who went on a shooting rampage for what seemed like no apparent reason? Maybe he was fired from his job and went back seeking revenge. Every time a reporter talks to one of his ex-coworkers, they describe him as nice, quiet, reserved and introverted. The underlying truth is that he allowed years of frustration, anger and perceived unfairness to build up.

People who take the blame for anything just to make another person happy go off the deep end.

And when they do lose control, someone ends up being the scapegoat because anger has built up inside them. A person who clams up in anger appears to have it together. It seems as if nothing bothers him. But the reality is that instead of releasing anger in a controlled manner, he lets the pressure build up until it comes out in an uncontrolled manner.

Men need to learn to talk to their wives when something happens to them. If you're having problems on the job, or it seems as if nothing is working out right, or there are financial problems, you need to tell your wife. She knows when you're upset, and she will ask if there's something wrong. Being open and honest with her doesn't make you less of a man. In fact, when you express your frustrations, your wife should be your biggest supporter. A supportive wife might say, "Don't worry about it, Honey. You are a child of God, and He will meet our every need. And if I have to work, I'll go to work, but we will not go under."

God didn't call the man to carry the load himself. God made us to communicate with that woman. If this wasn't God's intention, He would have left Adam by himself with the animals. We've got to learn to talk because if we don't, we'll be frustrated and take it out on our loved ones.

I (Mack) have learned not to cover up my feelings when something bothers me. I've also learned to be specific about what is confidential between Brenda and I as husband and wife. I've shared some personal things with Brenda that I considered to be confidential. However, when I shared these things I did not ask her not to tell them to others. Consequently, Brenda ultimately shared what I intended to be private. When I heard that she had shared these confidential matters, I got angry. But it was really my fault because I never expressed to her my desire to keep these things private. Then I clammed up because I thought she might share the fact that I got angry over the incident. In order to avoid these moments of anger, I have learned to verbally identify what I considered confidential between us as husband and wife.

A clam-up person deals incorrectly with anger by using the silent treatment. When he finally opens his mouth, he can come across as a know-it-all. He is a harsh critic of those around him, and his criticism comes with hostility, anger and bitterness. It seems as if nothing is ever good enough for him.

You Are Not a Robot!

There is nothing wrong with being a reserved person. There are some people who are quiet by nature. Mack is basically a quiet person, but given the right circumstances he will talk. It is when a person always isolates himself from those around him that he becomes dangerous. Isolation is the first step to destruction. Isolation breeds explosive anger which destroys everyone in its path. The problem of isolation has to be confronted with both people giving input and listening to each other.

Some people hardly ever seem to talk. Instead, they are likely to turn inward for protection. I

(Brenda) used to be this way. Anybody who knows me would never believe it, but really — I was quiet and introverted! As a girl, there were circumstances in my life that caused me to become introverted. I would come home from school in the evenings and do my chores. After doing my chores, I would lock myself in my room and read. I wouldn't socialize with anybody because I didn't want to be rejected or cause any ill feelings. I just wanted to be by myself. As a result, I became depressed and almost had a nervous breakdown.

People who don't acknowledge their emotions or feelings act like robots. They don't know how to interact or respond to others. God created within us the ability to feel and be passionate, but we are to exercise self-control.

People who clam up are usually perfectionists. When their perfectionistic demands are ignored, they become angry. This anger is the result of selfishness and immaturity on their part more than a reflection of misconduct on the part of the person who offended them. Saul often displayed this type of anger toward David.

> Now the distressing spirit from the Lord came upon Saul as he sat in his house with his spear in his hand. And David was playing music with his hand. Then Saul sought to pin David to the wall with the spear, but he slipped away from Saul's presence; and he drove the spear into the wall (1 Sam. 19:9-10).

Saul's jealousy of David led him to destructive anger because Saul was selfish. The tormenting spirit had its roots in jealousy, anger and pride, and it led to Saul's downfall. Saul's life was empty because he was satisfied by meeting man's expectations, not God's. His life was not one of righteousness, peace and joy in the Holy Ghost. Saul became angry when he saw God's favor and anointing upon David.

Whether we tend to blow up or clam up, the best thing we can do is surrender our anger to God, confess it and release it to Him. You may think, *Well that's easy for you to say! You don't have to put up with the nonsense I do!* We'll show you how surrendering, confessing and releasing anger to God can free you to love those you would otherwise hate.

THE KIND OF PEOPLE
YOU JUST LOVE TO HATE

Hate. That's a strong word. Did your mother ever tell you when you were a child, "Don't say you hate him. That's a terrible thing to say. God wants us to love everyone." Then as you walked away, you muttered under your breath, "OK, but I don't like him." Many people still do this as adults!

Most of the time, people who say they hate

someone don't really mean it. They're angry and caught up in the heat of the moment. However, hatred is such a powerful emotion that sometimes it drives a person to murder as it did Cain.

> Now Abel was a keeper of sheep, but Cain was a tiller of the ground. And in the process of time it came to pass that Cain brought an offering of the fruit of the ground to the Lord. Abel also brought of the firstborn of his flock and of their fat. And the Lord respected Abel and his offering, but He did not respect Cain and his offering. And Cain was very angry, and his countenance fell.
> So the Lord said to Cain, "Why are you angry? And why has your countenance fallen? If you do well, will you not be accepted? And if you do not do well, sin lies at the door. And its desire is for you, but you should rule over it" (Gen. 4:2-7).

Whether Cain's or Abel's sacrifice was bigger or better isn't the issue here. The point is that God saw the attitudes of their hearts. When we see someone else being rewarded and don't receive the same blessings, we become angry with the other person. Jealousy causes us to become angry with successful people.

As I (Mack) said in the introduction, I became angry with God and successful white ministers because I resented them. It wasn't until God revealed to me the attitude of my heart and told me He was going to bring me up to His standards that I was able to overcome these feelings and get the victory. We want the reward, but we don't want to make the necessary sacrifice to obtain it.

For example, a person who wants to be a doctor studies long, hard hours and continues studying long after he graduates from medical school. A good physician keeps abreast of the latest medical developments and technology.

His relatives, however, may resent him because they are jealous of his success. They feed off negative feelings instead of concentrating energies on their own personal goals. His relatives might say, "Now he thinks he's better than us. He thinks he's a big shot just because he's a doctor." What they don't realize is that he made the effort and sacrificed ten years (or more) of his life to become a professional. He's gone the extra mile and then some.

God warned Cain, "Sin lies at the door waiting for one small crack so it can creep into your life" (see Gen. 4:7). That crack can be anger. By asking God to help us get rid of the anger, we get rid of other negative emotions that are contagious and touch the lives of those around us.

> Now Cain talked with Abel his brother; and it came to pass, when they were in the field, that Cain rose up against Abel his brother and killed him. Then the Lord said to Cain, "Where is Abel your brother?" He said, "I do not know. Am I my brother's keeper?" (Gen. 4:8-9).

Cain's anger led him to murder Abel because Cain was jealous of Abel's blessing. As a child of God, expect people to become angry with you when God rewards you. They see God's blessing on you, and they become jealous. They want your blessing, but they don't want to offer the acceptable sacrifice to receive it. But be careful not to fall prey to the temptation of retaliation. Keep your heart pure before God. The Word of God says, "Pray for those who spitefully use you" (Matt 5:44) or are angry with you.

As we said earlier, let anger become a constructive power instead of a destructive power. Learn to say, "I'm going to do better." Don't get jealous of someone else's success. Find out what he's doing and allow it to motivate you into giving God your very best.

I (Mack) once jokingly said to a pastor-friend, "Just when I thought I was getting a bigger choir, you've increased yours by another eighty members." Instead of being jealous of him, I rejoiced with him. I allowed his success to motivate me more in the ministry.

When we're in a right relationship with God, we rejoice with a brother or sister in Christ who is promoted or recognized. If we don't rejoice with him or her, then we need to check our motives. The devil takes advantage of us when we're spiritually weak. Satan begins planting negative thoughts in our minds toward the other person. Don't give in to those thoughts. If we've done our best, then we can rejoice with our brother knowing God rewards those who walk uprightly (Ps. 84:11).

Finally, brethren, whatever things are true,
whatever things are noble, whatever things
are just, whatever things are pure, whatever things are lovely, whatever things
are of good report, if there is any virtue
and if there is anything praiseworthy —
meditate on these things (Phil. 4:8).

Putting these attributes into practice gives us
God's peace and prevents us from becoming angry,
jealous, bitter or hateful. When we fix our minds
on godly things, then we're able to cast down
every temptation.

IF YOU CAN'T TAKE THE HEAT...

Many people don't learn how to handle anger
because they hate confrontation. They deny their
feelings and believe everything will turn out right.
"I'm just going to turn it over to the Lord," they
say. But there comes a point when confronting a
situation or a person is necessary in order to be
delivered from anger.

Most men in the Western culture hate public
confrontation, especially when it involves a woman.
When a man gets into an argument with a woman,
he's going to look bad no matter what he says or
does. So the only thing he can do is sit there and
take the heat.

Often we men avoid confrontation with our
wives because we don't know how to verbally
communicate our feelings. Half the battle in overcoming anger with others and frustration with

ourselves is learning to communicate. For example, let's say a man's wife attempts to make fried rice for him, but she undercooks it. A man who knows how to communicate with his wife will say, "Baby, that was the best fried rice I ever had," even if the fried rice was green. He will reinforce her efforts with positive words instead of putting down her cooking abilities.

Women too need to learn how to communicate with men. One of the most important things men need from their wives is respect. So many young, American women are growing up without their fathers, and they are taught independence and aggressiveness from an early age. So when they're involved in a relationship or marriage and conflict arises, they blast that man because they haven't been taught how to communicate with men. No one has shown them that men like to be respected and admired by their girlfriends or wives.

As a woman dealing with men of various backgrounds, lifestyles and cultures, I (Brenda) have found respect is one area that is a common ground for all men (Eph. 5:33). When women can respect men, they will have fewer problems in dealing with them. Proverbs 29:20 tells us not to be rash with our mouths. Since women are more in touch with their feelings, they are better able to communicate and express what's going on. Men, on the other hand, need time and space to gather their thoughts before they can express their feelings.

Men hate to be put down in public places or in front of people. They want to feel as if they are in control of a situation. If there is a situation where the man and woman disagree, the woman should remain calm and take control of her thoughts and anger before she reacts to the man.

Once we were in a restaurant and a couple sat at the table next to us. They argued and got loud. The man was trying to keep everything quiet. He was real cool, but she was upset.

"I don't know what you think. You upset me!" the wife said.

"Shhh," he said.

"How could you do that? And you think I'm going to have dinner with you? You're nothing but a hypocrite!" she said.

"Are you going to leave me some money?" he asked.

She expressed how she felt, and she didn't care who realized it. The lady jumped up and took her money with her. The man sat there, really cool like nothing happened, just sipping water. About fifteen minutes later he slid out of his seat, strolled over to the door and eased out. He didn't have any money.

Another time we were getting on an elevator to go up to our hotel room. A lady came running down the hallway screaming, "Please protect me! Protect me from this man!" Brenda and I stared at each other. My driver and I said, "This man must be beating her."

"Please get him off of me; get him off of me!" she kept screaming.

Then we saw a man calmly following her path down the hallway. He got in the elevator behind her. It soon became obvious the man following her was her supervisor. Apparently, she had stolen the company books from a project she was working on, and he fired her. She was so angry that she retaliated by trying to publicly accuse him of harassment.

When he got into the elevator, she started kicking him! We tried to hold her back, but then she kicked us! I (Mack) felt like saying, "Go ahead and crack her, man!"

"Would you please give me those?" the supervisor nicely asked her.

"I'm not giving you anything! I earned these books!" she yelled at him.

If that lady had handled the situation differently, maybe things would have gone a lot easier for her. She could have said, "I was wrong. I see how you handled the situation, and I'm sorry I reacted that way. Please forgive me."

Even if you are wronged, be cool. Don't let your feelings cause you to lose it. The person who wronged you may change his tune if he sees you can handle the pressure. If a coworker or supervisor is spreading rumors about you, just keep your cool. The truth will all come out in the wash. God will make your righteousness shine like the noonday sun (Prov. 4:18).

I'M TELLING YOU THIS IN GOD'S LOVE

Earlier we showed you how Christ confronted people. There's a right way and a wrong way to confront people. The way we confront people will either draw them to Christ or push them away. A lot of people leave churches because of something that a church member or pastor has said or done to them. Confronting a brother or sister in Christ at the wrong time or in the wrong way causes offense among members.

Our attitude, how we look at people or how we say things to them, may offend them. We are held accountable for those we cause to stumble. We have a great responsibility to treat everybody equally before the Lord. God commands us to love all kinds of people.

Although God commands us to love everyone, we don't need to surround ourselves with people who are constantly bitter or angry. We can love them with the love of Jesus Christ, but if we're constantly around them, eventually we will become bitter and angry.

There is an old proverb that says, "Tell me who you associate with, and I'll tell you who you are." If we are surrounded by carnal people and things, our carnal man will grow faster than our spirit man. But if we soak our minds with the Word of God (Eph. 5:26), our spirit man will take over. When the fire gets hot, the Holy Spirit reminds us: "Be renewed in the spirit of your mind."

It might be that the angry person hasn't reached a certain level of spiritual maturity yet. Recognize when the enemy is trying to attack with anger and bitterness. If you hang out with people who seem to bring out the worst in you, then don't hang out with them anymore until they grow. Pray for them. If you confront people by giving them a piece of your mind, you will offend them for all the wrong reasons.

LET ME GIVE YOU
A PIECE OF MY MIND

Anger makes us hear all kinds of voices — the devil's, your flesh's and other people's: "If I were you, I would just tell them off"; "You need to just give them a piece of your mind"; "I wouldn't take that if I were you."

If we're not careful about giving someone a piece of our minds we may end up losing them! A lot of times we want to blame the devil. But we can't blame him because our flesh desires to blast someone as much as the devil want us to. Look at what Proverbs 29:11 says about giving someone a piece of our minds:

> A fool vents all his feelings, but a wise man holds them back.

Every morning you contemplate what outfit works best according to the weather and activities that day. You may think about it the night before. But if you're like most people, you blindly pull something out of the closet thirty minutes before you leave and say, "I think I'll wear this today."

Just as you dress every morning in the natural, you also need to dress in the Spirit. Put on the full armor of God every day (Eph. 6:13). This way you'll learn how to control what comes out of your mouth. If you don't, those words will have punch to them and move you into sin.

Many people feel they have a right to say whatever is on their minds. These people are never happy with anything. They thrive on arguing all the time. They like to argue just to hear themselves talk. Sometimes they argue because they're insecure, and arguing gives them the feeling of being in control. Like my (Mack's) mama says, "They just argue all the time. Some people will argue with a signboard." Here is a guaranteed formula to start an A-R-G-U-M-E-N-T with anybody:

A ACT AS IF SOMETHING IS WRONG, BUT INSIST IT ISN'T.

It shows a tremendous immaturity on our part when we act like babies. All we need is a pacifier. Many times women sense something is bothering their mate, boyfriend or friend and want to discuss it. A female poses such questions as, "What did you say that for?" or "What do you mean by that?" If the man doesn't want to discuss his problem or acknowledge that there's something wrong, he might try to brush her off.

"I didn't say anything. Just leave me alone! There's nothing bothering me!" But she sees his face changing the entire time she's talking to him. So she presses him for a response, and then he snaps. Instant argument.

R RELY ON YOUR EMOTIONS ALL THE TIME.

You reveal your temperament by your words — those spoken and those left unspoken. One of Jesus' disciples, Peter, is probably best known for having a bad temper. Peter's life was a prime example of what happens when our emotions run rampant. Peter was a zealous man who relied on his emotions many times. In Matthew 16:22-23, Peter chastened Jesus for predicting His death, and in turn, Jesus rebuked Peter for trying to postpone the inevitable. Later on we see the same passion displayed when Peter cuts off the guard's ear in Gethsemane (see John 18:10-11). But probably the biggest emotional struggle Peter faced was his denial of Jesus.

> Now Simon Peter stood and warmed
> himself Therefore they said to him, "You
> are not also one of His disciples, are
> you?" He denied it and said, "I am not!"
> One of the servants of the high priest, a
> relative of him whose ear Peter cut off,
> said, "Did I not see you in the garden
> with Him?" Peter then denied again; and
> immediately a rooster crowed (John 18:25
> 26).

Peter was on an emotional roller coaster. One minute he was telling Jesus he would never deny Him (see Matt. 26:35), and the next minute he was denying him! The gospel of Luke records that the Lord turned and looked at Peter. What a look that must have been from our Lord Jesus! It was then that Peter remembered Jesus' words, and he went out to weep bitterly (see Luke 23:61). Peter thought that it was too late to correct a wrong. But he later repented and was reconciled with Jesus.

How many times have we allowed our emotions to run away with us and get us into trouble? Nothing is ever solved when we rely on our emotions instead of trusting God. Allowing our emotions to take control causes our imaginations to run wild. For example, we immediately jump to conclusions that so-and-so hates us or gives us dirty looks. Maybe we think our mate doesn't love us anymore because he or she is too quiet. Instead of jumping to conclusions and getting emotional, learn to ask God for guidance and then approach the situation.

6 GET DEFENSIVE WHEN SOMEONE MAKES A SUGGESTION TO YOU.

Some of us don't like criticism even if it is constructive. A good litmus test for constructive criticism is that if it's coming from two or three different sources, you can bet your bottom dollar it applies to you. Its source may be a friend at work or at church or a lifelong friend. A person who is truly a friend will confront us at times. Probably the hardest confrontations are those from a spouse. Because of the intimate relationship between husband and wife, we know each other's strengths and weaknesses.

When somebody confronts us, we need to learn not to take it personally and to be mature enough to receive what they're saying in a positive manner. We need to pray about them and not wear a chip on our shoulders. Ask God to help you handle criticism better so that these confrontations don't cause strife.

A few years ago, I (Mack) invited some consultants to give us some expert advice on how we could improve our television format. Their suggestions stunned me because they involved changing the decor of the stage area as well as upgrading our present equipment.

I received their advice with mixed emotions because I had finally decorated the set the way that I had dreamed. As they explained how we needed a warmer, softer decor, I felt anger and resistance growing within me.

It took me a few days to deal with my pride and

accept the team's recommendations. With Brenda's help, I concluded that they were the experts in the field — not me — and was able to receive their advice without getting angry and upset.

U Use every opportunity to get your own way.

Recently Brenda and I had an intense discussion regarding our vacation plans. We try to schedule a vacation for us as a couple and then a vacation for the whole family. During this discussion, I (Mack) brought up the point that on our couple vacations Brenda always seems to go where she wants to — shopping and more shopping. My argument was that I very seldom get equal time in a quiet, solitary place of rest.

This discussion went back and forth until the volume level of our voices increased. At this point I usually close down completely rather than discuss the issue any longer. I know I have entered a realm where Brenda is most comfortable — verbal exchange. She is in touch with her feelings and can discuss them without getting angry. If I continue to exchange words at this point, I am most likely to clam up until the discussion is back in verbal zone and away from the feeling zone.

After I meditated on this issue for a while, I realized that Brenda — along with my three other professional shoppers (my daughters) — give a lot of time to assist me in the ministry without one complaint. We ended the conversation by recognizing how we both give to each other in different ways. We decided that equal time would be given to each other's desires by dividing the days for individual favorites. For instance, one day we may go shopping and the next day we may go to the beach or do some other activity. Being sensitive to one another's needs guards us from using every opportunity to get our way in our lives and marriages.

M Misinterpret the words of other people and read into their actions.

Some people read too much into the meaning of what people say or do to them. They are angry because they've been hurt in life. Men and women handle anger differently. For example, suppose a woman's car breaks down, and she walks to the nearest pay phone to call the pastor.

"Pastor, my car broke down, and I don't know what to do. Please come and get me!" she says, hysterically crying.

"Now Sister, calm down. It's gonna be alright. How far are you from the church? Where are you?" the pastor asks her.

"I'm about an hour away from the church. Come and get me! I think I'm just gonna die out here!"

"Is there a relative that lives nearby? Please tell me where you are, and someone here in the office will find you a ride."

"No, Pastor! I want you to come and get me!"

"I can't go personally because I'm in the middle of solving another crisis, but I'd be happy to send someone from the church to get you. Please, just tell me where you are."

"I can't believe this! What kind of a pastor are you! Here I am in need, and you don't want to help me!" And she slams the phone down.

She jumped the gun and assumed the pastor didn't want to help her. But the truth is he wanted to help her; he just couldn't rescue her personally. Most people know that pastors are very busy people, but they don't understand how busy. In the ministry, you'll have situations like this one almost daily. And because of gender differences, it's important to learn how to control anger.

> Like a city whose walls are broken down
> is a man who lacks self-control (Prov. 25:28, NIV).

Brenda and I have found that the higher up you go in God, the stronger the wind factor is against you. We've learned not to take it personally when people come against us in the ministry. Do what Jesus said, "Father, forgive them, for they do not know what they do" (Luke 23:34). If we are wrong, we ask for forgiveness. Ask God to help *you* to change.

E EXPECT THE WORST OF PEOPLE.

People who like to argue look for the worst in others. A newly born-again Christian may have come from a drug or alcohol background. But now the person has given his or her heart to Christ. An angry, argumentative person expects the worst from someone with that kind of past. He thinks, *This ain't going to last.* This type of anger leads to a judgmental attitude toward others and as a result, we position ourselves to be judged (Matt. 5:22). The right thing to do is to display agape love and see the saved sinner through the eyes of Jesus. The apostle Paul says:

> Therefore let us pursue the things which make for peace and the things by which one may edify another (Rom. 14:19).

Speak positive words to people and about people. How often have we heard, "If you can't say something nice about someone, don't say anything at all"? By speaking positively, you're speaking blessings into their lives.

N NEGLECT MEETING THE NEEDS OF ANOTHER.

We need to put ourselves in the other person's shoes. As we become sensitive to his or her needs, we're filled with compassion. But when we always see things from our own point of view, it's difficult for us to understand the other person's feelings.

Men, have you ever been left alone with the kids on a Saturday? You couldn't wait for your wife to come back home. That one hour seemed like eight hours. Why? Because you were in a situation that you aren't used to being in. I (Brenda) bet it gave you a much better understanding of your wife.

Sometimes a man becomes angry with his wife when she will not sexually fulfill him. Suppose your wife became handicapped or quadriplegic or developed a disease and couldn't fulfill your physical needs. What are you going to do? Are you going to go to another woman? No! As men, we need to exercise self-control. Instead of becoming angry with our wives, we've got to be sensitive to their needs and recognize when they are tired or don't feel well.

I (Brenda) want to say to the wife that having an understanding husband is no excuse for you to withhold yourself. There may be times when you don't feel emotionally or physically capable of giving to your husband. But even if you're angry with him or angry about something else and your energy is zapped, withholding yourself from him is wrong. Real love is not selfish or manipulative — it's sacrificial. As a married woman, you are not your own anymore (1 Cor. 7:3-5).

In some cases, the woman has been violated and needs to release her anger and frustration. Maybe you've been abused. You need to release your anger to God. Father God gave you His Son, Jesus, to carry all your pain, burdens and anything you have ever gone through so you could be set free.

Even if your husband is not the most sensitive, caring and tender person in the world, you are the one who needs to release the anger. Do you get mad at your husband every time he gets near you? The truth is you're not angry with him; you're angry with the person who violated you. You may take it out on him because every time he does come around, his actions bring back those bad memories. The only way you can overcome this obstacle is to release your feelings and the perpetrator to God.

As husbands, we need to ask God for an extra dosage of patience, sensitivity and understanding. If you love your wife as much as you say you do, you'll forgive her. Learn how to minister to her emotional needs and be tender with her. Abide in the presence of God, and He will guide you.

T TELL OTHERS ANYTHING THAT PUTS THEM DOWN.

Have there ever been times when you felt great until somebody said one comment to make you feel bad? Maybe you went to visit relatives and no sooner had you stepped through the door then they started in on you. Don't snap back at them. Instead, kindly excuse yourself and leave. Tell them, "I'm sorry you're having a bad day. Maybe I'll come back another time." This way you don't get into an argument and get out of the Holy Ghost.

We live in a negative world. We can listen to just ten minutes of the evening news and feel like somebody dumped trash in our minds. If we look at the wrong talk show for thirty minutes, we begin to mistrust everybody. We are left with feelings of hopelessness.

Sometimes we say things in the heat of the moment. We should be careful not to tell our spouse or parents in anger, "I hate you," or "I don't love you anymore." Or tell our children, "I wish you had never been born. You're embarrassing." We don't really feel that way toward them. The truth is we don't approve of what they said or did. It takes a long time to overcome harsh words, and a spoken word cannot be taken back. For each negative comment a person receives, it takes a dozen positive comments to counteract it. But the person, particularly a female, will hold on to those words. Whether the person forgives you or not, it will be a long time before that person trusts you again.

There are some words that not even time can erase. Those words leave emotional wounds that only Jesus can heal. Claim the Scriptures, "He shall give His angels charge over you" (Ps. 91:11) and "No weapon formed against you shall prosper" (Is. 54:17). It's important that we measure our words carefully and speak to people as if Jesus were speaking through us.

Avoiding arguments with those we're closest to can be a difficult feat to accomplish. In the next chapter, we'll show you how to break any spirit of bitterness between you and your family — both your natural and spiritual families.

EIGHT

MY BROTHER'S MIDDLE
NAME IS SANDPAPER

Every day you will cross paths with someone who does things differently than you, and you may get aggravated by them. Whether it's your mate, children, ministry partner or coworker, eventually their aggravating differences will lead you to anger if you allow them.

BLOOD IS THICKER THAN WATER — AND IT BOILS QUICKER TOO!

Early in our marriage, I (Brenda) remember going to brush my teeth and finding that Mack had squeezed the toothpaste tube in the middle. His habit made me angry, and I verbally attacked him.

"Why did you squeeze the toothpaste in the middle like that?" I asked.

"That's the way I've been doing it all my life," Mack replied. Then we argued back and forth.

I said, "Well, then it's time for you to change. I don't like my toothpaste tube to be squeezed in the middle."

"When did it become your toothpaste?" Mack asked.

"When I married you."

"No, it didn't become *your* toothpaste. It's *our* toothpaste."

"Yes, but what's yours is mine."

"Let me ask you something. Could you get any toothpaste out of it?"

"No, I couldn't because you squeezed it in the middle."

"Let me show you how to squeeze it in the middle and get toothpaste out of it."

"No, I don't want it like that!"

I was too immature to overlook the fact that Mack squeezes the toothpaste tube differently. Another of Mack's habits I had trouble overlooking was his untidiness. I came home to find clothes strewn on the floor, making a path that eventually led me to Mack.

"Did you see you left some clothes on the floor?" I asked.

"I'm going to wear those again tomorrow so don't put them away," he responded.

"Then why don't you pick them up and put them in the drawer since you're gonna wear them tomorrow? I didn't marry a child; I married an adult! Didn't your mama teach you how to pick up after yourself?"

"Don't get my mama into this now!"

Mack's untidiness would aggravate me. I (Brenda) was thinking, *This is a grown man. He needs to pick up after himself.* And I (Mack) was thinking, *If she would just give me a break, I would come back to get them.* (That's right; I'd come back the next day when I'd put them on.)

I (Brenda) was angry with Mack because I felt as if my rights were violated. Here I had spent time cleaning the room only to go back and find clothes on the floor. All my energy was wasted. I had a choice to allow this to bother me or to go behind him and pick them up.

A man feels the same way about his automobile. Maybe his wife drives his automobile and hits a mud puddle. Maybe she tries squeezing it into a parking space and the people in the car next to her open the door, leaving paint marks and dents on the car. He can choose to get angry, or he can say, "I'm just glad you didn't run into the side of a mountain."

Some things, such as bringing drugs into the house, should not be overlooked. But if a man drops his clothes on the floor, just pick them up.

85

Sometimes we get out of line with our relatives, friends, coworkers, church family and even complete strangers. Unbridled anger is immaturity or selfishness on our part. If a person doesn't respond the way *we* want him to or do things *our* way, we let him have it with both barrels.

Learning how to deal with relatives regarding touchy issues can be challenging. Because we know each other's weaknesses as well as strengths, we will constantly argue unless one person is mature enough to overlook the other person's shortcomings. The Word of God says that sometimes He allows difficult people into our lives to smooth out our rough edges.

> As iron sharpens iron, so a man sharpens
> the countenance of his friend (Prov. 27:17).

Jesus had His challenge with His domestic family. Because the Bible doesn't mention Joseph, Mary's husband and Jesus' earthly father, during the ministry, crucifixion and resurrection of Jesus, it's assumed he may have passed away, leaving Mary a widow. It seems that Jesus had been left "holding the bag" when it came to her well-being. The question comes to mind, *Where were the other sons and daughters that were born to Joseph and Mary?* (see Matt. 13:55-56).

During biblical times, just as the oldest received the birthright, he was also responsible for the care of an elderly or widowed parent.

While Jesus was still talking to the crowd,

his mother and brothers stood outside,
wanting to speak to him. Someone told
him, "Your mother and brothers are standing outside, wanting to speak to you." He
replied, "Who is my mother, and who are
my brothers?" Pointing to his disciples,
he said, "Here are my mother and my
brothers" (Matt. 12:46-49, NIV).

Jesus' earthly family seemed to lack an understanding of the purpose of His ministry. However,
Jesus remained focused on His assignment from
God for that time. The Lord Jesus made provision
for His mother's needs before He died on the cross
by assigning the apostle John to take care of her.

Now there stood by the cross of Jesus
His mother, and His mother's sister, Mary
the wife of Clopas, and Mary Magdalene.
When Jesus therefore saw His mother,
and the disciple whom He loved standing by, He said to His mother, "Woman,
behold your son!" Then He said to the
disciple, "Behold your mother!" And from
that hour that disciple took her to his
own home (John 19:25-27).

God has used several family situations to mature
us in Him especially in the area of forgiveness.
God is well aware when we go the extra mile with
our relatives, and He will multiply our seeds of
kindness back to us in this lifetime. Paul wrote to
Timothy concerning the daily care of widows.

> But if any widow has children or grand-
> children, let them first learn to show
> piety at home and to repay their parents;
> for this is good and acceptable before
> God (1 Tim. 5:4).

Even though in today's society the responsibility
weighs upon all the children to share the load to
care for a parent, this is sometimes not possible.
The entire load may fall upon one child because
the other children are unable or unwilling to cooperate. Sometimes the one child may be the parent's
only child. In either case, anger and resentment
may come upon the child left to care for the parent. The child may feel trapped and the parent, at
the same time, doesn't want to become a burden
to the child. And some families have a spirit of bitterness or a spirit of anger assigned to them which
compounds the problem. Unless someone discerns
this and breaks the curse, touchy family issues will
only cause that spirit to grow stronger.

But you can be the family member that breaks
the cycle. When you receive Jesus Christ, the curse
is broken. You determine if the curse stays in your
family. You can say, "The curse stops here."

We have found that when there is conflict
among relatives and we pray with fervency, God
has a specific answer. He is a rewarder of those
who diligently seek Him (Heb. 11:6). We have
never suffered loss if our motive is to live peace·
ably with all parties involved.

Sometimes couples or families need Christian
counseling. We're not saying line up at the door

for counseling. But in some situations couples or family members may need to share their feelings because they can't come to a happy medium. They need to seek outside counsel. Otherwise unresolved issues will cause the family structure to crumble.

I'VE GOT YOU UNDER MY SKIN

If you're involved in part-time or full-time ministry, watch out for people who get under your skin. The enemy will try to move you into discord with someone who has a similar anointing or calling. Satan specializes in creating friction, conflicts and anger among people with similar talents, abilities or callings in the body of Christ.

Satan's main goal is to produce competition among those who would otherwise team up and become more effective as well as learn from each other. It's like a baseball team that gets into a fight in the dugout before the game begins. Agreement is a threat to the devil because there's power in agreement (Matt. 18:19-20). So his goal is to stop agreement by creating strife or competition among people.

If you are a pastor, the devil's goal is to create suspicion, anger, mistrust and competition between you and another pastor in the area. If there is a leader with a similar mission or calling upon his life, the devil will attempt to get you suspicious of each other instead of working together as a team to produce a fruitful harvest.

Unfortunately, much of the hurt and distress in

the body of Christ has come from others who call themselves Christians. We once heard the testimony of a former witch tell how witches attack churches that have the potential of reaching their communities.

This person said that witches place priority on casting spells toward the pastor and his wife with the hope of causing a divorce. Then they try to destroy the church's vision by planting themselves in the church leadership. Unless there is constant prayer and intercession in the church for unity, this normally results in a congregational split.

> Now I plead with you, brethren, by the name of our Lord Jesus Christ, that you all speak the same thing, and that there be no divisions among you, but that you be perfectly joined together in the same mind and in the same judgment. For it has been declared to me concerning you, my brethren, by those of Chloe's household, that there are contentions among you. Now I say this, that each of you says, "I am of Paul," or "I am of Apollos," or "I am of Cephas," or "I am of Christ" (1 Cor. 1:10-12).

Paul had some big problems in the Corinthian church. The enemy had infiltrated the church through a spirit of division. People were beginning to credit and praise man for their salvation instead of lifting up the name of Jesus. Paul was trying to tell them, "Look, we're not here to build a fan club. We're here to build the kingdom of God." We see the same problem in the church today. Often we hear and see people who join or leave churches because of the minister. Jesus said in John 12:32, "If I am lifted up from the earth, I will draw all peoples to Myself." If more churchgoers remembered these words and prayed for the church leadership, we would have fewer church splits.

Many of us do know God's Word, but when it comes to practicing the Word so the world can see spiritual fruits in us, we don't. People who display the fruits of the Spirit and love others are a joy to be around.

Although a person may be able to quote scriptures backward and forward, the true strength of his spiritual maturity is how he gets along with other people and how they get along with him.

Some people don't understand the order of authority or how to deal with authority. Jesus gave us the prime example of submission to His heavenly Father's authority.

> During the days of Jesus' life on earth, he offered up prayers and petitions with loud cries and tears to the one who could save him from death, and he was heard because of his reverent submission. Although he was a son, he learned obedience from what he suffered and, once made perfect, he became the source of eternal salvation for all who obey him (Heb. 5:7-9, NIV).

91

Many people get a curse on their life when they break the line of authority in trying to straighten something out. There's an order to doing things.

CONFRONT IN LOVE

In chapter 6 we said that confrontation can be necessary. As pastors, sometimes we have to confront people, and that doesn't make us number one with them.

Paul had to confront a situation involving an incestuous relationship in the church at Corinth because the leaders ignored it. Paul was angry with the leaders about their apathy. He was grieved in his spirit and cried many times over the situation. Paul suppressed his feelings as long as he could, but the time came when he had to deal with it.

> But I determined this within myself, that I would not come again to you in sorrow. For if I make you sorrowful, then who is he who makes me glad but the one who is made sorrowful by me? And I wrote this very thing to you, lest, when I came, I should have sorrow over those from whom I ought to have joy, having confidence in you all that my joy is the joy of you all. For out of much affliction and anguish of heart I wrote to you, with many tears, not that you should be grieved, but that you might know the love which I have so abundantly for you (2 Cor. 2:1-4).

Over the years we have had to confront situations in our church. There have been times when an unmarried man and woman who were newcomers in the Lord were living together. So we lovingly gave them the Word of God, discipled them and showed them how to live a godly life. Some couples recognized they were in sin and repented. But others said, "You know, we don't see anything wrong with it. We're going to get married anyway around the year 2000. Can't we just stay together and warm up?" And we answered with an emphatic no and showed them scripturally why it's wrong. Most of the time they got mad and left the church.

> Remember those who rule over you, who have spoken the word of God to you, whose faith follow, considering the outcome of their conduct...Obey those who rule over you, and be submissive, for they watch out for your souls, as those who must give account. Let them do so with joy and not with grief, for that would be unprofitable for you (Heb. 13:7,17).

Whether on the job or at church, know the house rules. For instance, if I (Brenda) go to a church and the rules are no bright colors, no makeup and no pants, then I should submit to the authority and abide by those rules. If I choose to go there, then I have placed myself under the authority of the church leaders. If I usurp their

93

authority and ignore the house rules, I make myself vulnerable to being attacked and becoming angry with them.

If I walk out mad it's my fault because I chose to expose myself to that environment. Now I've copped an attitude. People sometimes get angry when their supervisor tells them to do something. But their supervisor is not forcing them to stay in their jobs. If they don't like what the supervisor requires of them, then they can hit the door. Otherwise, they need to zip their lips and stay in love. They want the money, but they're not willing to cooperate.

Whether it's a blood brother or sister, a brother or sister in Christ or a fellowman, we can learn to confront in love and be a godly witness. We will see next how the pressure of dealing with people and difficult situations will make you a better person.

WHEN PRESSURE IS
PRESSURING YOU

Everyone enjoys a good back rub. When I give Brenda a massage (and I had better be careful with my big hands on her little shoulders!), the nerves in my fingertips have a sensitivity to the pressure points in her muscle so that I know how much pressure I should apply. If I apply too much pressure, I could hurt her. If I apply too little pressure, the massage won't help alleviate the muscle tension.

In the spirit realm, life's pressures produce a tension inside your spirit. Pressure is not necessarily bad for you; it's how you deal with it. It doesn't matter whether pressure comes from an expected project, a deadline on the job or the unexpected death of a family member. It's how you handle the pressure that either makes you a mature person or stunts your spiritual growth.

Webster's dictionary defines pressure as "the burden of physical or mental distress; the constraint of circumstance; the weight of social or economic imposition." People under pressure either suppress or repress their emotions.

I define suppressing anger as taking authority over your emotions for a while and then responding to the situation. You defer taking action on a situation without losing touch with the problem. On the other hand, repressing anger means to bury your feelings indefinitely or to prevent the natural or normal expression of anger. By not confronting the situation, you eventually become unaware of the fact that you're angry. You become numb to feeling any emotions.

By repressing our anger, we may say something we later regret. But as we become Spirit-controlled, the Holy Spirit helps us suppress our anger for a short time to prevent us from saying hurtful words.

ARE YOU A PEACEMAKER OR A NEHEMIAH?

Usually people who repress their anger consider themselves peacemakers. They don't want to rock the boat. But they don't realize that by not discussing what's bothering them, they're only making the situation worse. Some who consider themselves peacemakers misinterpret the meaning of the fruits of meekness and gentleness. They've misinterpreted these fruits to mean repression when they actually mean self-control.

> But the wisdom that comes from heaven is first of all pure; then peace-loving, considerate, submissive, full of mercy and good fruit, impartial and sincere. Peacemakers who sow in peace raise a harvest of righteousness (James 3:17-18, NIV).

Learn to express how you feel and still keep the peace. Say something such as, "What you said upset me. I'll have to think about that." This is a good way to suppress your anger and avoid starting a war.

Anytime you try to do something great for God, the devil will oppose you and bring negative pressure into your life. When Nehemiah and the people of Israel rebuilt the city walls, they met with some opposition and pressure in pursuing the building project. The city officials persuaded the king to place high taxes on the people, convinced that the financial burden would lead the people to abandon the project. Also, the high taxes resulted in the rich Jews taking advantage of their poorer brothers.

About this time there was a great outcry of protest from parents against some of the rich Jews who were profiteering on them. What was happening was that families who ran out of money for food had to sell their children or mortgage their fields, vineyards, and homes to these rich men; and some couldn't even do that, for they already had borrowed to the limit to pay their taxes.

"We are their brothers, and our children are just like theirs," the people protested. "Yet we must sell our children into slavery to get enough money to live. We have already sold some of our daughters, and we are helpless to redeem them, for our fields, too, are mortgaged to these men."

I [Nehemiah] was very angry when I heard this; so *after thinking about it* I spoke out against these rich government officials (Neh. 5:1-7, TLB, italics added).

Nehemiah didn't just run out and start chopping heads off — no. Although he was angry to hear about the wrongs committed against the people, he took some time out to think about what he was going to say. After Nehemiah spoke with the rich Jewish officials, they restored to each man his property and his children, and then they canceled the debt (v. 12).

As you read this book, maybe you are experiencing what you believe to be an injustice committed against you or someone you love. Maybe you were passed up for a job promotion and someone less skilled than you got it. Perhaps you're involved in a ministry, and church folk constantly criticize you and call the pastor to complain about everything you do "wrong." Maybe you're trying your best to please your mate and no matter what you do, he or she is never satisfied.

We become angry because we feel our rights are denied or stepped on. God has given us the freedom of choice, but as Christians, everything we have — our rights, gifts, talents, loved ones and so on — belongs to God (1 Cor. 6:19-20; Rom. 12:1). You may have every right to feel angry, but remember: You can choose to control how much you will allow pressure to get to you. Get into the Word, suppress the anger for a while, and let God handle it. Learn to concentrate on God's will and purpose as well as His promises. One healthy way to suppress anger is through prayer. Say a simple prayer such as:

> Lord, help me to see this issue Your way.
> Help me to sort out my feelings and do
> the right thing. In Jesus' name, amen.

What helped Nehemiah get through the tough spots was not only the fact that he thought before he spoke but also that he was constantly shooting "arrow prayers" to God (Neh. 1:4; 2:4). He was in touch with Father God, and his spirit man was in control.

WHEN PRESSURE BURSTS YOUR BUBBLE

Sometimes a person can't perceive pressure in the natural, but it does exist in the supernatural. Unless he knows how to release that pressure, it will keep building until he blows up. Often too much pressure leads a person to commit suicide, or if married, leads to a separation or divorce. Without God's help, the result of pressure is destruction.

Suppose I (Mack) gave four people inflated balloons and told them to pop them. The unexpected popping sound of the balloons bursting is startling and can be painful too.

People under pressure act like inflated balloons. They explode unexpectedly and scare people away. They don't even know they're under tension and stress. Their way of venting pressure is to go around biting people's heads off. They come across harsh and don't even know it because they've allowed pressure to build up inside them. If we make any noise, we had better make a joyful noise unto the Lord (Ps. 98:11).

When we succumb to pressure and explode, what comes out doesn't sound good and the results aren't good either. There are certain recognizable symptoms and characteristics that will indicate to us that we are venting pressure the wrong way.

1. Our conversation will likely take on a critical nature toward others. We complain more than praise others.

2. The creativity in our job performance or life goals comes to a standstill.

3. Many people go to the extreme in their eating habits. They become over-eaters or do not eat enough nutritious foods.

4. Insomnia is another sign that pressure is winning the battle over perfect peace in our lives.

Dr. Lester Sumrall, a beloved leader in the body of Christ who recently passed away, once stated to us that he could look at the way a man walks and tell how far that individual is going in life. It is true that our body language is often a telltale sign of what is going on inside of us. Our angry thoughts can be detected through a look of disgust or a lack of expression. If one's expressions are seasoned with slander, humiliation, gossip and sarcasm, the root is most likely anger.

Sometimes Christians have the mentality that because they have given their lives to God, they're free from problems and pressures. That's a lie. From the moment you commit your life to Jesus Christ the devil is out to destroy you. He hates not having control over you anymore.

> Many are the afflictions of the righteous,
> but the Lord delivers him out of them all
> (Ps. 34:19).

The word *afflictions* means "pressure, tribulation, persecutions, distress, pain, offense" and so on. Afflictions and pressure will come, but you've got to be strong. You've got to have resilience. You've got to have buoyancy.

Crisis brings pressure, and many of us don't know how strong we really are until pressure is applied. For instance, if Brenda tries to exert pressure on my hand and I'm pushing back with all my strength, she's going to move back because I'm stronger than she is. But if Brenda is established in righteousness, nothing will shake her.

> In righteousness you shall be established;
> you shall be far from oppression, for you
> shall not fear (Is. 54:14).

By becoming established in righteousness and allowing it to shine through your life, you keep oppression away. You're like a strong tree planted by the rivers of water (Ps. 1:1).

Pressure makes us stronger in the Lord. If we have the Word of God in us, we're going to bounce back from the pressure. No matter what kind of pressures attack us in life, we've got to be persuaded that He will deliver us out of them all. With God's Word and His help, we will find the way out. Pressure won't overtake us because greater is He that is in us than he that is in the world (1 John 4:4).

PUT THE MONSTER BACK IN THE CAGE!

Picture this: You're in church, you're hungry, and your stomach starts growling — Grrrrrr! Can you do anything about it? No, not really. You wouldn't just start eating in the middle of a service, would you? No, because it's not right. But your body is telling you, "I'm hungry, and you had better do something about it now." So what do you do? You push your stomach in and eat a mint or chew gum to keep it from growling. You control it, right? Now, if your stomach were in control, you would get up, go out and get something to eat. But because it wouldn't look nice to leave in the middle of the service, you sit there.

This fact about our stomachs helps us understand the spirit man and the carnal man. Unless you feed on the Spirit, the carnal man is going to control the spirit man. Whoever is active in you will take over. When pressure causes us to lose control, it brings out the worst in us. Learn to put the monster back in the cage! The Word of God says He will keep in perfect peace whose mind is stayed on Him (Is. 26:3).

It's your choice whether or not you allow pressure to move you into uncontrolled anger. Even in uncontrollable situations you can have the mind of Christ and harness uncontrolled anger.

TEN

CONTROLLING YOUR ANGER IN UNCONTROLLABLE SITUATIONS

It's 6:00 P.M., and you're stuck in traffic. You still have to pick the kids up from day care, get them something to eat, and go home and get ready for midweek service which starts at 7:00 P.M. The problem is that you're fifteen minutes away from the day care. "I'll never make it on time," you say. And today of all days, you get all the slowpokes in front of you (immediately men say, "Women drivers!"). So you pop in your *Celebrate Jesus* tape hoping it gets you in the Spirit, but the same lips that are trying to praise God can't resist hurling insults at the driver in front of you. Sound familiar?

> With it [the tongue] we bless our God and Father, and with it we curse men, who have been made in the similitude of God. Out of the same mouth proceed blessing and cursing. My brethren, these things ought not to be so (James 3:9-10).

As long as you are breathing, there will be situations in your life over which you have no control. You have no control over who was your father or mother. You have no control over the family you were born into or the color of your skin. God orchestrates these things.

Learn to release the anger, resentment and bitterness if your parents are not who you thought they should be or were not responsible for you. Don't try to compensate for what your parents didn't do.

If you assume your parents' role and responsibilities, it will keep you from doing what you should do. If you realize that there are some situations in which you have no control, right then and there you will get rid of a lot of anger.

You can choose to become angry over uncontrollable situations, or you can allow the peace of Christ to rule your heart and life (Col. 3:15).

> Now listen, you who say, "Today or
> tomorrow we will go to this or that city,
> spend a year there, carry on business
> and make money." Why, you do not
> even know what will happen tomorrow.
> What is your life? You are a mist that
> appears for a little while and then van-
> ishes. Instead, you ought to say, "If it is
> the Lord's will, we will live and do this or
> that." As it is, you boast and brag. All
> such boasting is evil. Anyone, then, who
> knows the good he ought to do and
> doesn't do it, sins (James 4:13-17, NIV).

If Jesus Christ is the Lord of our lives, then we
cannot change the past, present or future. We cannot change our family background, our family
members or the way others perceive us. Whatever
comes our way, good or bad, is subject to God's
providence and divine order for our lives. If He
truly is in control of our lives, then why become
angry because things are not going the way we
want them to? When we commit our plans to God,
His purpose for our lives will ultimately be fulfilled. Let's look specifically at how to deal with
various uncontrollable situations.

RACISM: LEPROSY OF A DIFFERENT KIND

Our society is plagued with racism. Many of the
wars going on in the world today are due to racial
tension. Many times people are despised and
treated like lepers because they speak a different

language or because of their skin color or nationality. When Jesus was on the earth, He encountered prejudice and hatred from those who were not of the Jewish race. One such example is found in Luke 9:51-56.

> Now it came to pass, when the time had come for Him to be received up, that He steadfastly set His face to go to Jerusalem, and sent messengers before His face. And as they went, they entered a village of the Samaritans, to prepare for Him. But they did not receive Him, because His face was set for the journey to Jerusalem. And when His disciples James and John saw this, they said, "Lord, do You want us to command fire to come down from heaven and consume them, just as Elijah did?"
>
> But He turned and rebuked them, and said, "You do not know what manner of spirit you are of. For the Son of Man did not come to destroy men's lives but to save them." And they went to another village.

As we said earlier, racial differences stood as a barrier between the Samaritans and the Jews. When the Samaritans saw that Jesus was intending to go to Jerusalem after He was to minister in one of their villages, they did not receive Him or His disciples.

Jesus rebuked two of His disciples, James and

John, who had fallen victim to hatred and prejudice and wanted to command fire to come down and consume the Samaritans. As we saw through the illustration of Jesus and the Samaritan woman in chapter 3, the living water we receive from Jesus gives us His ability to love all races of people and become bridge builders in life.

We have witnessed strong barriers of prejudice in the hearts of black people against white people in addition to seeing and experiencing prejudice of white people against black people. Only the transforming power of Christ can cause us to love each other as equals.

THE PAST: A SITUATION THAT REQUIRES CONFRONTATION

Much of our anger arises when we have unrealistic expectations as they relate to the opposite sex. We get disappointed when plans and relationships don't go as we would like them to go.

Some men have put all females in the same category, thinking because they had a domineering mother that all women are domineering. Some women have put all men in the same category. Because they've had a bad marriage, they think all men are louses. Judging a current relationship based on a past relationship gone sour prevents us from receiving God's blessings. This happened to a couple we once gave premarital counseling to.

We were so excited when two particular members of our church began to spend time together and expressed an interest in marrying each other.

Both of them were divorced with children from previous marriages.

In our counseling sessions with them, they seemed like mature Christians who had overcome hurts and disappointments and were ready to go on with life. The issue of repressed anger and offense never surfaced during the sessions.

During the honeymoon, a discussion arose between them that sparked a fuse of their past relationships which was very unpleasant to each partner. They both reacted as if they were talking to their former mates. The outburst of anger and quarreling that took place was such that they never were restored. Even after much counsel and encouragement not to give up on the marriage, there remained irreconcilable differences. The repressed anger surfaced at the slightest resemblance of past offenses. Learn to monitor the character of each individual and to treat each individual as just that — an individual, not a ghost from the past.

UNCONTROLLABLE FAMILY SITUATIONS

While completing this book I (Mack) had a fresh encounter in my own life with anger that arose from a family situation beyond my control.

In addition to our four children, we also keep our niece, who is a beautiful girl. She has been with us almost a year, and we have allowed her mother, who is single, regular visits approximately once a week. On the day papers were to be signed for us to have custody her mother had a change of heart, and our niece was taken from our home and returned to her mother.

This action deeply angered me. I had a dramatic change in my personality, and it was noticed by my family. They heard me expressing my anger in a loud, verbal way to Brenda. One of the things that ignited my anger was that we faced a similar situation with a nephew a few years ago. The recent incident along with the former experience had struck a fire of emotions in my soul.

I called a family forum to explain how I was feeling about losing our niece and how it had brought back emotions from the incident with our nephew. After an hour discussion, we ended the meeting with prayer. The prayer time truly freed me from the anger I was feeling about the situation and toward the people involved in removing our niece from our home.

After experiencing this loss, we were motivated to pursue adoption. We wanted to direct our anger toward a constructive effort, so we began required training for certification as foster parents and adoptive parents.

As a result of allowing anger to propel us to become certified for foster care and adoption, our niece was returned to us one month later! Our relationship with her mother has been restored, too. A hearing for custody is scheduled very soon.

When anger is controlling your life, look for ways you can prevent the destructive anger from dominating your every thought and action. When we determined to do something constructive with our anger, God gave us the desire of our hearts concerning custody of our niece.

HEY GOD! WHERE ARE YOU?

Have you ever prayed and not gotten a response when you thought you would — not even in the year you thought you would? You cried out to God and said, "Are You up there? Have You gone to sleep or what? Do You see what I'm going through?"

At one time or another, everybody has felt his prayers were falling on deaf ears. It seems as if you pray over and over, and God doesn't answer your prayers in the way *you* think He should or when *you* think He should. But sometimes God has a greater purpose and destiny in not answering your prayers in your time or your way. Look at one person's testimony of how he overcame his anger with God.

A few years ago I became angry with God over what I felt to be unfair treatment by a coworker (I'll call him Bill), my supervisor's indifference to the situation and a lack of response on God's part to rescue me from the situation.

Have you ever met a person who rubs you the wrong way? Well, somehow Bill's personality and ways seemed to do just that. Bill and I worked on numerous projects together and, as with any project, communication between those coordinating its various tasks is a must. I often kept Bill abreast of the status of the tasks, but Bill would take the facts that I relayed to

111

him and express them in written reports or during meetings in a light favorable to himself. If he made a mess of things, I had to go back and fix the problem.

After various projects, I became frustrated at Bill and angry with God for repeatedly allowing me to have to clean up Bill's oversights. God began dealing with me to hold my peace, do the extra work and pray for Bill. But despite praying for him, I began to react to his verbal jabs and became confrontational with him in business meetings. I prayed "Lord, move me or move Bill." God did neither. Instead, God showed me that I would be called into full-time ministry, but first I had to learn how to deal with this situation. When I complained to God about Bill's lying, He would respond, "Stop confronting him and hold your peace." I thought God was so unfair. I was frustrated. God wouldn't do anything, so I felt compelled to protect myself.

Finally it sunk in — I was coming up short in the love area! God had sent Bill in my life to show me the limits I had put on His love. I repented and released my anger toward God and Bill. Now I realize that God was testing the depth of my love for Him and for Bill. Today I am in full-time ministry just as God had spoken to my heart.

Thank God this individual was able to work through His anger with God and his coworker. But there are those individuals who get so angry with God that they become bitter toward Him. It eventually leads them to completely sever their relationship with Him because they think that by pouting, they're punishing Him. But God can't and won't be controlled by whims and temper tantrums.

David was once angry with God because his prayers went unanswered. So he wrote God a letter to vent his frustration.

> How long, O Lord? Will You forget me forever? How long will You hide Your face from me? How long shall I take counsel in my soul, having sorrow in my heart daily? How long will my enemy be exalted over me? Consider and hear me, O Lord my God; enlighten my eyes, lest I sleep the sleep of death; lest my enemy say, "I have prevailed against him"; lest those who trouble me rejoice when I am moved (Ps. 13:1-4).

But by the end of the letter, David had calmed down; he had cooled off. David moved from anger to rejoicing.

> But I have trusted in Your mercy; my heart shall rejoice in Your salvation. I will sing to the Lord, because He has dealt bountifully with me (vv. 5-6).

David dealt with his anger and got rid of it. From verses 4-6, we can see that David's attitude changed. He had an attitude check. David started the letter angry with God; then he worked through his feelings and finally calmed down. Remember when we first discussed Ephesians 4:23, "Be renewed in the spirit of your mind"? David was getting his mind back on God.

Even if you do become angry with God, the key to overcoming the anger and accepting God's answer is washing your heart with the Word. Once you begin fellowshipping with God and getting your heart lined up with His Word, your heart begins to melt.

Learning to accept the unexpected and uncontrollable will help you bring your anger under control. In the next chapter, we'll show you how to deal with displaced anger.

ELEVEN

LEARNING TO COUNT TO TEN — OR TO ONE HUNDRED

You've had a long, hard day at work. As you're walking out the door your supervisor hollers, "Why didn't you finish that project? You've missed the last two deadlines! If you miss one more, you're fired!" Reluctantly, you turn around and stay late to finish the project. On your drive home you start honking the horn at the driver in front of you who is poking along. The driver doesn't know that you're angry because your supervisor made you stay late. After a one-hour trek, you come home to find the kids eating junk food before supper and fighting with each other. At the height of your frustration, you let them have it with both barrels. The kids go outside and vent their frustration by kicking the dog. Now everybody is in a bad mood — even the dog! — and the cycle continues the next day.

Many times we don't know how to harness anger's energy much less deal with it in a positive way. This unresolved anger becomes displaced anger. If Mack said something to upset me yesterday, and we've not resolved the issue, then when I wake up I'm still going to be thinking about it today. And I'll have another bad day. If we continue to ignore it, I'm still going to think about what he said days ago. This can go on for weeks, months, even years. People who don't let go of past hurts hold grudges over things that were said years ago.

It's important to learn to talk about what makes you angry and deal with it before the day is over (Eph. 4:26). You may not be able to talk about it at the moment. But let your temper cool down — count to ten or fifty or one hundred — until you can speak in a soft voice. Be swift to hear, slow to speak and slow to anger (James 1:19).

HEAPING COALS OF FIRE

You can do something about your anger whether

or not the other person apologizes. Every bit of anger, vengeance or bitterness you hold on to sidetracks you from walking in God's love. Sometimes people will come against you or despitefully use you, or the devil will use people to attack you. Satan's goal is to get you out of God's love so you won't achieve what God has for you.

Paul says in Hebrews to lay aside every weight of sin (12:1). Every person that you don't forgive is like a weight around your neck. Lay aside the weight of unforgiveness by heaping coals of fire on your enemy's head (Rom. 12:20). You might think, *Heaping coals on my enemy sounds like taking revenge.* Actually, the opposite is true.

In the Bible lands almost everything is carried on the head — water jars, baskets of fruit, vegetables, fish or any other article. In many homes the only fire they have is kept in a brazier which they use for simple cooking as well as for warmth. They plan to always keep it burning. If it should go out, some member of the family will take the brazier to a neighbor's house to borrow fire. Then she will lift the brazier to her head and start for home.

If her neighbor is a generous woman, she will heap the brazier full of coals. To feed an enemy and give him drink was like heaping the empty brazier with live coals, which meant food, warmth, and almost life itself to the person or home needing it and was the symbol of finest generosity.[1]

You heap coals of fire on the other person's head by forgiving him and by displaying agape love. If Mack and I have a conflict, I should go to him whether it's my fault or not. If I go to him and say, "I'm sorry, would you please forgive me?" and also forgive him, then I have freed myself from the bondage of resentment and bitterness. If he chooses not to forgive me, then he's the one carrying the weight. But I'm free because I've dealt with that issue, and I've cast my care on God.

People may offend you and not even know it. In fact, most people that you get angry with don't know that you're angry with them. Forgiveness simply means deciding to no longer carry a grudge. If you say, "I've got a right to feel this way, and I'm going to hold on to these hurts for the rest of my life," then you're only hurting yourself.

As we said earlier, forgive and forget. Realize that the Lord has forgiven you of many things, and decide to operate in forgiveness. As the Bible says, "To whom much is given, from him much will be required" (Luke 12:48). Although you forgive the offender, it doesn't mean that he is free from the consequences of what he did. God will deal with that person, but forgiveness sets you free.

GET A TUNE-UP

Do you ever wake up in the morning with your spiritual motor running rough, and you don't even know why? Maybe you had a bad dream the night before, and when you woke up, the first thing on your mind was how someone mistreated you on the job.

If you leave the house angry or in a bad mood you will carry that attitude throughout the day. Get a tune-up. Sometimes all it takes is one Bible verse to get back on course. Meditating on the Scriptures puts you in the right spirit. By meditating on the Scriptures, you begin to walk in the Holy Ghost, and He will guide you during those trying times.

Years ago when Mack would get really mad, the Holy Spirit would tell me to jump on his back and start tickling him — and I would.

I would tell Mack, "I'm sorry. Honey, whatever it is I did, I ask you to forgive me."

"You don't even know what it is?" Mack would reply.

"No. Tell me what I did to make you angry."

"First, you didn't cook what I asked you to cook. I told you to have..."

"OK, but you called and told me at five minutes to five, and I try to have your food ready by six."

"I don't know what it was you put on that plate, but it was lumped on there. What's the use of a man working if he can't even eat what he wants?"

"Honey, I asked you ahead of time what you wanted for next weekend, and you said, 'I never had a choice growing up, so I don't need a choice now.' I ask you to forgive me."

Then I'd start tickling him. Somebody in the household has to have the mind of Christ to keep peace. If you're a single parent, sometimes the kids can get on your nerves. But if you're walking in the Holy Ghost, you have the power to walk in love. Ask for it!

COUNT TO ONE HUNDRED; THEN DON'T SPEAK

As loving as Mack and I seem, we're still growing. We're constantly monitoring how we react and respond to our children. We have four children, one of whom is a teenager. Everybody knows that teenagers go through changes in life. Women and men in their thirties and forties go through changes, too. If you have teenagers and people in midlife crisis living under the same roof, you could have a real explosion. So somebody's got to have the mind of Christ!

If I (Brenda) get angry with Mack, I will go to him and say, "Honey, I'm sorry. I was tired, I was feeling bad, and I took my frustration out on you. Therefore, it's really my fault. I'm sorry I even said all those things to you. Please understand that I really didn't mean to say those things. I was talking out of fatigue."

Most of the time Mack is a lovely person. But there are those few times when he's not so lovely. I know not to even look at him. I'll leave him alone and say to myself, *Now, Brenda, he's been in the office all day counseling people aside from having to make one decision after another.* If your husband makes one decision after another, he may not be too pleasant when he comes home.

Most men need a little break in between.

For instance, if I (Brenda) have been home all day without a soul to talk to, I may strike up a conversation with Mack as soon as he walks through the door. But if he's tired, he may not feel like talking.

I ask Mack, "So, Honey, how was your day? Anything happen today?"

"No, nothing! OK?" Mack says.

"Who did you see?"

"I didn't see anybody."

"OK. So nothing happened, and you didn't see anybody."

I know not to ask any more questions. I immediately try to have the mind of Christ and find out what I can do to help him relax. Normally a cool, tall glass of lemonade helps him relax. Or if I go over and say, "Honey, let me loosen your tie," or "Honey, can I take your shoes?" he loses his edge.

Learn to count to ten in dealing with displaced anger. In doing so, you become more sensitive to the voice of the Holy Ghost. As you minister to those around you, it will be only a matter of time before you see the power of gentleness operating in your life.

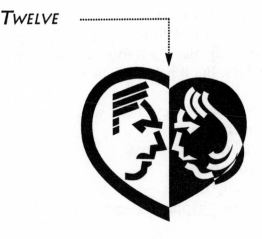

TWELVE

THE POWER OF GENTLENESS

It was summertime. The camp counselors gathered the children together for the annual camp play. This year it was about Noah's ark. The counselors picked a five-year-old girl to play the part of the lion, but they chose the wrong kid. The night of the play, she made her way to center stage to recite her one-liner. Fear and panic struck her little heart as she looked out at a sea of unfamiliar faces. In a soft, coy voice she murmured, "And the lion roared."

Some compare gentleness to weakness, passivity, powerlessness or timidity. But gentleness is actually a strength that's needed in order to have another fruit of the Spirit called self-control, or temperance. The Greek word for *gentleness* is *epieikia.* It means "fairness, moderation or sweet reasonableness" in actively dealing with others.[1] It is the quality of having control over our emotions so that we express anger in the right way and for the right reasons. That is, it means to be kind, even-tempered, refined in character and conduct. In Philippians 4, Paul says, "Let your gentleness be known to all men" (v. 5).

The nature of anger acts as a gauge to indicate how much we have grown in the fruits of the Spirit. We think we're spiritually mature until we get angry. Then we realize we don't behave any differently than before we were saved. Satan tempts us to get angry and say things we don't mean, and we fall right into his trap. The words come out so fast and then the devil accuses us by saying, "I thought you said you were saved."

Accusing us is Satan's specialty. He is the accuser of the brethren (Rev. 12:10). Memorize scripture and use it to refute his accusations and condemnation. When we want to curse somebody or retaliate, the Word will come out of our mouths because it's in our hearts. "Out of the abundance of the heart the mouth speaks" (Matt. 12:34).

If we don't hide the Word in our hearts, we remain immature — babes in Christ. But God wants us to grow up in Him. As the psalmist said:

> Your word have I hidden in my heart, that
> I might not sin against You (Ps. 119:11).

The devil works hard to sow discord between husbands and wives, people at church and coworkers. He works overtime to tempt us to become angry and stay angry. Anger causes us to miss the blessings of God because it closes the heavens. So when the thought to be angry enters your mind, cast it down. We have to constantly cast down every evil imagination (2 Cor. 10:5) and allow the love of God to rise up in our hearts.

Suppose I (Brenda) came home from church and Mack started arguing with me. I sense that I'm getting angry, but if I'm in the right spirit, I'll recognize that Satan, not Mack, is attacking me. The Word of God says we do not wrestle against flesh and blood. Immediately I can say, "Oh no, devil. I know your strategy. That's not Mack acting; that's you. You're not going to steal my blessings. I cast you down in Jesus' name." The Bible tells us to submit to God, resist the devil and he will flee (James 4:7). We have to react this way with people we love and don't love, those we know and those we don't know.

Sometimes we're angry, and we don't even know why. We feel warm on the inside, but it's not a fuzzy warmth. It's the kind of heat we feel when all the blood rushes to our heads.

One characteristic of an angry voice is aggressiveness. An angry voice sounds rash and harsh.

It's a voice of vengeance. But underneath that voice is a still, small voice in our minds that says, "Take it easy. Be cool, and simmer down. Walk away, and get out of here." That still, small voice moves us away from anger.

The tone and volume levels of our voices increase when we're angry, and our voices project out. A word to the wise: Lower your tone of voice two notches instead of raising it. As we say in our book, *Lifesavers for Your Marriage*, "The tone of your voice will determine whether the content of your words will gain entry into the ear of the listener (1 Cor. 16:14)."[2] This truth applies not just in marriage relationships but in all relationships.

> If anyone considers himself religious and yet does not keep a tight rein on his tongue, he deceives himself and his religion is worthless (James 1:26, NIV).

Sometimes if I (Brenda) have a bad day at the office I simply need to talk about it. And I, like most women, tend to elevate my tone of voice a little bit when I'm frustrated. Mack listens to me gripe and helps me to lower the tone of my voice. Sometimes he'll say to me, "Honey, it's going to be alright." He lets me know how much he appreciates me and gets my mind off the thought that maybe I'm not appreciated at work.

The same is true for men. Your husband may come home from work and say, "You know, I did all the reports today, and I'm going to have to redo all of them tomorrow. I work so hard, and nobody appreciates me."

There are times when Mack comes home down-hearted, discouraged and feeling unappreciated. I make it a point to encourage him. "Honey, I appreciate you, and I read those reports. I thought you did a great job." By reinforcing his value to me with positive thoughts, I get him out of the anger and bitterness stage. Then he is able to maintain his objectiveness and evaluate the situation as a whole.

Here are some clues to keep in mind when pressure builds up:

1. DON'T USE PHRASES THAT PLACE THE BLAME ON THE OTHER PERSON ONLY.

Correction is rarely received. If you're confronting someone choose your words wisely. You don't hear many people say, "Just go ahead and correct me. I'm ready for any kind of rebuke." That's difficult to confess. The word *bitterness* comes from the word *bite*. You can take the bite out of what you're saying by knowing how to say it. For example, don't use phrases such as: "You always do..." or "You never do..."

Those are phrases that really put wood on the fire. One of the best ways to verbalize your feelings is by expressing it in first person. You can say things such as "I feel like" or "This is the way I feel when you do such and such." In our book, *Heaven on Earth in Your Marriage,* we discuss using "the sandwich effect" when correcting someone.

> Start by saying something good. Then tell your mate the problem or situation. Allow

them to express themselves. If you come into agreement immediately, that's great. If not, conclude with "Let's just pray about it," and a kind remark concerning how good it is that the two of you can discuss what is bothering you. Faithful are the wounds of a friend; but the kisses of an enemy are deceitful (Prov. 27:6).[3]

We applied this principle to the marriage relationship, but this communication technique works well with anyone under any circumstance. When correcting someone, do so in a positive manner. Constructive criticism builds up the other person without tearing down his self-esteem.

You reap what you sow. If you sow softness, you reap softness. If you sow hardness, you reap hardness. That's why you need to control your anger. If you say, "I'm going to whip you," you'll get whipped yourself. When I (Brenda) get angry with Mack, I make sure I pray before approaching him. This way I don't give place to the devil. I'll tell Mack, "Honey, I'd like to talk to you about something and express my feelings about a situation." By expressing my feelings, I'm opening the door so that he too can express himself without becoming defensive. But if I attack him during the conversation, he has a fair chance to attack me.

There have been times when I (Mack) said something in anger to Brenda, and after I said it, I ended up acknowledging that I was just as much at fault. At first I felt it was all her fault. Anger will make you magnify someone else's fault and ignore your own. But because she's able to maintain a soft attitude and can speak to me in love, by the end of the conversation I'm able to recognize my own faults.

2. Change your physical surroundings.

Sometimes changing your environment helps you not to become angry or bitter. I (Brenda) remember when we entered into full-time ministry, I was accustomed to working every day. When our daughter, Christanie, was a baby I stayed at home with her. Mack would come home and say to me, "Honey, why don't you go to the mall?" He was sensitive to my needs although I wouldn't have said anything. But he wanted me to be in a good frame of mind, so he would get me out of the house.

Take a minivacation from the situation. If you stay in the same, stressful environment too long you become prone to abusive behavior toward those around you. Child abuse and spouse abuse occur at the hands of someone who is under constant pressure without an outlet. If you have problems in your life and you start abusing your child, your mate or anybody else, you will be in big trouble with God. Using your hands to slap or hit someone upsets God. He didn't give us hands to abuse people; He gave us these hands to lift them in praise to Him (Ps. 134:2).

I (Mack) remember once chastising my oldest child, LaNica. I've whipped her maybe twice in her whole life. As I went to whip her, I remember her saying, "Daddy, what is that fire in your eyes?"

That was the last time I ever whipped her. I had let the anger build up inside of me, and I lost control. For a long time, she would walk past the room where I was sitting and stare at me, but she wouldn't come near me. It was a terrible feeling knowing that my daughter was afraid of me, and God judged me for my actions.

Now what does that tell us about our relationships with others? Anger will cause us to do and say things in a way that we will later regret. Most people don't really want to abuse their spouse or children. But if they don't get a break, they vent their uncontrolled anger on their spouse or children, and it puts up walls in the relationship. Remember, we said that when you're angry your face expresses it.

In my (Mack's) situation with LaNica, my anger showed in my eyes. Although I was not physically abusive to LaNica, my uncontrolled anger caused a breach of trust between us. It was years before she felt comfortable coming to me.

As a married woman in full-time ministry, I (Brenda) often need a break. The demands on me as a wife, mother and minister are enormous. At least I have my family and people in the ministry who love and support me. I can just imagine what single moms go through! If you know of a single parent who is struggling and under tremendous pressure, offer to give them a break by baby-sitting (for free) one evening. Maybe invite them over for dinner or cake and coffee. As Christians, we need to be sensitive to one another. We should remain in a prayerful attitude so that whenever we come in contact with someone, we know how to minister to him or her.

In the workplace, try to change locations during lunchtime. Don't eat lunch at your workstation. Even if it's doing something as simple as walking outside and sitting under a tree, change your atmosphere so you can mellow out a bit.

3. HAVE A HOBBY, AN OUTING OR AN EXERCISE PROGRAM TO RELIEVE THE STRESS.

Most stress-free people are those who participate in sports. You may relieve stress by swimming, exercising or doing yard work. Maybe you like to window shop — just don't buy anything on credit, or you might become stressed out again! Make it something that is not a normal part of your daily routine.

Vacations are important because they get your mind off work and change your environment. If possible, try to plan two vacations a year — one for both of you as a couple and one for the entire family. As we said earlier, Brenda and I plan these two kinds of vacations every year. As a husband, you may not have the financial means to take your wife on that second honeymoon to Hawaii. But even if you make reservations at a nice hotel in a neighboring city for a weekend — without the kids — you'll find out she's not as mean as you thought. She won't be as tired either — especially if the hotel is next to a mall!

Have a little fun in your home. Play with your children; play with your spouse. It gets out a lot of anger caused by anxiety and stress. When the child is small, take time out to play with him or her. Show your children how much you love them. Emotionally, that child will be whole. When a child doesn't receive affection and affirmation, there is an emotional deficiency in the child.

An emotional healing takes place when a father touches a child — especially a female child. Many young women who lacked the loving touch of a father are lured into a wrong relationship later in life. As they grow up, they're drawn to any man that touches them because their fathers didn't show them affection. They're confused about the difference between real love and sex. The man she has sex with may not necessarily love her, but it's the act of touching that makes her think it's love. So she ends up pregnant, has a baby out of wedlock and goes right back into that cycle.

Dads, please ask God to help you be a real dad. A real dad is one who expresses love to his wife, lets the kids see him expressing that love and expresses love to the children.

Whether we are dealing with our own frustrations or helping someone to overcome theirs, it's important to display the gentleness of the Holy Spirit. In the next chapter, we will give you eight steps to put a lid on anger that's about to erupt.

THIRTEEN

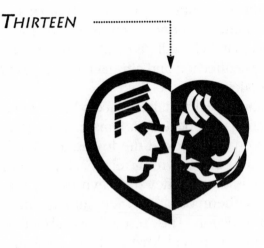

EIGHT STEPS
TO OVERCOME ANGER

Men and women often see things differently.
A lack of understanding about how we each
approach life can leave us frustrated and produce
feelings of anger. An incident in our personal lives
helped me (Mack) to walk through the eight steps
to overcoming anger that we will outline for you.

When we began ministering full time in 1979, I

(Mack) did most of the speaking during worship services, seminars and conferences. In 1984, God told me to bring Brenda up on the platform with me to preach because He wanted me to be held accountable in the eyes of the people. Brenda is a very expressive individual. As a result, the congregation would watch her reactions to what I was sharing from the pulpit.

This one act of obedience has given credence many times to our ministry as people watch our attentiveness to what each other is saying while ministering. Our unwavering attention to each other when ministering or teaching would send the message to the observer that we both agree. As a husband and wife ministry team, we would take turns preaching and speaking in marriage seminars.

We agreed that each of us would take thirty minutes to discuss a certain topic. As a man, I'm normally much more time conscious when it comes to an assignment of this nature. But Brenda is a natural communicator, and often she would just be getting to the topic at the thirty-minute mark. Inevitably, her delivery would pass the thirty-minute time limit, and she had no idea she had gone over. I often argued with God about how unfair it was to minister with a partner who seemingly had no sensitivity to timing.

Matters got worse if she shared some key points that *I* was going to make in my speech or teaching. Afterwards, she would readily apologize in order to keep peace between us. But after this scene repeated itself more than once, anger began to arise within me.

My anger intensified when Brenda would go off on a tangent. We had studied together, outlining the key points that mainly I had written. After we made the first point on the outline during our teaching, her teaching would be — in my opinion — considerably off course.

By this time, I had lost my joy. I concluded that I had to effectively deal with my growing anger toward God for asking me to allow Brenda to minister with me. I also had to deal with my anger toward Brenda for going over her time limit, using my key points and not being able to stick to an outline that, from a woman's perspective, had very little appeal. It wasn't until I overcame my anger by walking through these eight steps that I sensed God's peace about the situation.

1. RECOGNIZE YOU'RE ANGRY.

First, I had to *recognize* that anger had manifested itself in my life. I would occasionally voice my displeasure about what was going on when we spoke together. But when it seemed as if the discussion might lead to a confrontation between us, I would just clam up. I was denying what was really in my heart and naming it something else so I could avoid being labeled as having "the problem."

The best method to deal with my anger would have been to say, "Brenda, the fact of the matter is that it makes me angry when you consistently go over your time limit." Or I could have said, "Brenda, I feel so angry when you outtalk me ten to one when we are speaking."

To know Brenda is to love her. She is one of the most vibrant and delightful people in the world. She is full of excitement and loves fellowshipping with people. And because of her expressive nature, she is often aggressive when she communicates. In some instances when I am asked a question, Brenda will unintentionally answer before I can say a word. When I bring this to her attention, she quickly apologizes.

There were times that it would anger me when these "you-answered-before-I-could-say-anything" exchanges would erupt. For a while, I would just play them off as if they really didn't bother me. The moment came in my walk with God when I recognized my anger in this situation and expressed it to Brenda.

Admit that you're angry; don't deny it. Recognizing that we're angry matures us so that we no longer live in falsehood and denial about our true feelings over things that anger us.

> If you are angry, don't sin by nursing your grudge (Eph. 4:26, TLB).

When the step of recognizing anger is avoided, we no longer speak the truth about how we really feel (see step 6).

2. IDENTIFY THE CAUSE OF YOUR ANGER.

One of the reasons that God gave me Brenda was to make me aware that as a wife she can express her opinion without being labeled disrespectful or rebellious. As a man, I didn't realize that I had labeled expressive women as rebellious women. So when Brenda would radically express her opinion, subconsciously I would get angry and then express my displeasure by saying, "You never listen to what I'm saying because you're talking so much."

As a family, we have had the privilege of moving to new locations several times over the years. One of the biggest challenges to packing and moving is figuring out what is concealed in those boxes when you're finally unpacking. It's the same with anger. Without prayer and godly counsel, it can be difficult to identify the cause of our anger.

Our present reactions can be the result of something that took place years ago. When we mistake the cause of our anger, the anger becomes misdirected and displaced, causing a chain of negative reactions in our surroundings. To know how to handle your anger, you must properly *identify* the cause of your anger. Ask yourself questions such as:

- Why am I getting angry?
- Is it worth getting angry over?
- Will getting angry change the person or situation?
- Is my anger rooted in bitterness, resentment, hatred or any other fruits of the flesh? And if so, do I need to forgive someone or forgive myself?

If you're still having trouble identifying the root of your anger, pray and ask the Holy Spirit to reveal to you the source of the problem. By asking yourself some questions to help identify your anger, you're able to take the next step: evaluating the legitimacy of your anger.

3. EVALUATE THE LEGITIMACY OF YOUR ANGER.

Most college students become more serious during exam week. Every student knows that in order to be promoted and graduate, they must study and pass the exams. The phrase "burning the midnight oil" becomes a reality while preparing for the evaluation. When Brenda and I were in college, we would see students in their dormitory rooms, exchanging notes and reviewing the materials taught by the professors or instructors. Every student's dream was, *If only I had the answer key to the exam!*

Just as a good student must learn the professor's teaching style as well as their evaluation style in order to pass the course, so we must learn how to evaluate the legitimacy of our anger. Much of our anger can be misdirected especially if we don't properly evaluate the cause and source of our anger. In the *evaluation* stage, ask yourself:

- Do I have a justifiable reason for being angry?
- Is my anger the result of my own immature character?

To get to the source of my (Mack's) anger, the evaluation of my inner feelings would produce one of the following thoughts:

- I am angry because Brenda said this or that to me.

- She interrupted me while I was talking to someone else.

- Brenda didn't follow my suggested outline while we were teaching together.

- Could it be I'm just tired and need a day of rest?

The key to what we feel and why we feel that way is revealed during the evaluation stage. The attitude and motive of our hearts become clear as we *evaluate* what we are feeling as well as seeking to understand the heart of the individual or persons who have offended us.

The evaluation stage enables us to determine if we will allow God to deal with our inner spirit and develop character in us. Often during the evaluation stage we are trying to determine how we will confront the other party or parties about their actions toward us. The apostle Paul tells us in Romans:

> Therefore let us pursue the things which make for peace and the things by which one may edify another (14:19).

As pastors we have had to evaluate our hearts

when certain situations would arise in ministry. True pastors give their lives to teach, counsel, pray, visit, mentor and lead. There is a bond of love for the members that only God can give to pastors.

Over the years we have had members leave the church to go to another church or start their own ministry. Some members are cordial and inform us ahead of time of their desire to attend another church. Others quietly stop attending our church.

As senior pastors of Christian Faith Center in Creedmoor, North Carolina, we think we have one of the greatest congregations and ministries in the world. We struggle with mixed emotions over every departing member. But our greatest hurts come from those who quietly leave the congregation without a word — spoken or written. There is always some sadness when relocation or displeasure requires a member to change his membership.

In some cases we as pastors feel the pain of rejection and spiritual divorce when members leave our assembly. A covenant relationship is established between the pastor and the individual when the right hand of fellowship is given, inviting the person to become a member of the church. We think, *Why would anyone want to leave?*

True pastors love their congregations and give their lives, time and energy for the congregation. It is important that we allow God's healing power to restore our broken hearts so that we won't hurt those who remain at the church. Through prayer and meditating on God's Word we are able to evaluate each situation and stay in the love of

God. This way we can minister to the people who remain in the church without hurting them or offending them because of our past incidents with other members.

4. SUPPRESS YOUR ANGER.

Women are very good at perceiving things. Brenda can always sense when I'm upset about something, and she will look for an opportunity to ask me, "What's wrong, Honey?" I know that once I start the discussion, Brenda will continue to probe the issue, and that makes me angry. Over our twenty-five years of marriage there have been times when I (Mack) would say, "I just don't want to talk about it now," or "Nothing, Honey. I'll be alright." It's statements like these that raise a woman's curiosity even more unless the real answer comes forth.

Sometimes we hurt the people we love the most because we fail to suppress our anger until a time when we can speak the truth in love. There is a difference between suppressing anger and repressing anger as we outlined for you in chapter 9. Because men are more apt to respond physically at the height of our anger, it's a good idea if we men leave the scene and take a walk until we've calmed down.

Before learning how to suppress anger until I calmed down, I would speak forcibly about what was on my heart. The amazing thing is that Brenda often had no clue what she did or said that would make me so angry. She was just being herself. I've learned that I can bridge the time by saying, "What you said or how you said it did upset me, but give me some time to think about it before we talk further." This has been an excellent way to suppress my anger.

Don't allow anger to be bottled up or take root in you (Heb. 12:15). Learning how to suppress anger for a season is an act of maturity and an important step in controlling it. Once you learn to suppress your anger, the next step is to take the situation to God in prayer.

5. PRAY ABOUT THE SITUATION.

Almost 100 percent of the time when I (Mack) pray about something I'm angry about, no matter how right I think I am or how much I justify my thinking, God always deals with me first. Why? Because I'm the one who really needs the help. If I'm feeling angry and I've repressed it, God knows I need to deal with it.

Because men and women perceive things differently, it is vital that we pray *before* communicating our feelings. When we are angry with another individual, we need to focus our prayer on how to effectively communicate what we feel in a way that is pleasing to God. When we pray, God's power is active to lead us in every way. The Holy Spirit aids us in identifying what we feel as well as how to communicate our feelings. He helps me to answer the question: "Is it what Brenda said to you, or were you already uneasy about not achieving some other expectation?"

In a male/female relationship, we men are at ease when we are in control of the conversation. We are competitive by nature. And when we are confronted by aggressive and confident women, we usually will either become more aggressive in speech or get completely quiet to avoid a confrontation.

Prayer helps me to see the situation through Brenda's eyes and not become defensive when she makes a suggestion or expresses her opinion. Once you've prayed about the situation, you're ready for the next step: informing the person why you're angry with him.

6. INFORM THE PERSON OF WHAT MADE YOU ANGRY.

Now I'm ready to discuss the issue with Brenda and speak the truth in love. I've recognized my anger, identified its source and evaluated what made me angry. I've suppressed it for a short time and prayed about how to speak the truth in love. Now I can inform her of my true feelings.

"Brenda, it really bothers me when someone asks me a question and you answer it before I can say a word," I may tell her.

"Honey, I'm sorry. I thought the question was directed to both of us. I'll try to be more sensitive next time," Brenda says.

Usually, this answer doesn't appease my anger in the moment. But I know deep down that this is just Brenda's character and behavior. She doesn't mean any harm. Brenda's uniqueness and sweetness have an awesome impact on helping me forget the past and look forward.

When we recognize our anger and begin to express our true feelings to another, we must choose our words wisely. Be quick to commit to working out a solution. A workable solution considers the needs of all parties involved.

During the *inform* stage be absolutely certain that you calm down first and lower your voice. Without these two suggested steps, you are likely to create a situation in which both parties will increase their anger!

When informing another person about what made you angry or how he made you angry, be prepared to listen to his response. This is his opportunity to inform you of your offensive actions or words. Remember, it's more important to know how to handle disagreements than to win arguments. God desires for us to tell the person what we feel and confront the person, not his personality. We cannot change another person's behavior, but we can change our behavior with God's help.

When the offender is not present or you cannot make contact with the person, then write your feelings out rather than taking the chance of saying the wrong thing. Sometimes it's good to write things out.

7. FORGIVE AND FORGET.

As a husband and wife ministry team we have learned to exercise forgiving and forgetting toward each other so that God continues to bless what we do in His name. As we have grown in the things of God, we have realized the importance of being quick to forgive. When we don't forgive, we break the laws of God concerning relationships with others.

> And whenever you stand praying, if you have anything against anyone, forgive him that your Father in heaven may also forgive you your trespasses (Mark 11:25).

There are times in our lives when we all, to some degree, fail to hit the mark. Forgive the offender. The ability to forgive and forget comes from God. Most of the struggle to forgive takes place in the mind. Ask God to help you have a pure heart towards those who might have hurt you or angered you. "A sound heart is life to the body" (Prov. 14:30). Our health often depends upon our ability to forgive others and forget their offenses. Unless the heart is cleansed by forgiving and forgetting it will entertain evil thoughts.

> Bearing with one another, and forgiving one another, if anyone has a complaint against another; even as Christ forgave you, so you also must do (Col. 3:13).

Satan specializes in replaying memories of your past failures, pains, disappointments and hurts. Without forgiveness operating in your life, you will become selfish, bitter, resentful, cruel and insensitive, and you will develop an uncaring attitude and a hard heart. Jesus said that when we hold a grudge, we open our lives to tormentors (Matt. 18:34-35). Start by praying,

> Father God, I choose to forgive [person's name] for their actions and behavior toward me. I surrender to You all my hurts, pain and disappointments and I release [person's name] to You, in the name of Jesus, amen.

8. RESOLVE NOT TO LET THE SITUATION ANGER YOU.

Even if Brenda and I had been unable to find a solution, I was resolved not to let the situation get me into uncontrolled anger. The word *resolve* means "to make a firm decision about something" or "to cause one to arrive at a decision." Make your decision based on the Word of God. Let God be the One to "get even."

Abraham faced a situation with his nephew that required great resolve. Strife arose between Abraham's herdsmen and Lot's herdsmen over the land. But instead of becoming angry with Lot, Abraham resolved not to allow discord to come between them. Instead, Abraham humbled himself and allowed Lot to have first pick of the land. Abraham told him,

> If you take the left, then I will go to the right; or, if you go to the right, then I will go to the left (Gen. 13:9).

This showed great humility on Abraham's part,

because as the head of the family Abraham could have ordered Lot to take a certain part of the land. Abraham's humility strengthened his resolve not to allow anger and strife to divide the family. Humility looks to unify rather than criticize.

A number of years ago some of our church members began attending a Bible study held in the home of another member who happened to be a former minister. We were deeply hurt and angry when we found out that the Bible study was growing into a ministry. We thought that we had developed a friendship with the home group leader. We invited the person to speak at our church to show there was no jealousy or competition between us. Eventually, circumstances led us to require those attending the Bible study to make a decision about whether they wanted to remain members of our church or continue to follow the leadership of the other minister.

When approximately thirty or more of the members decided to follow the minister and start another church in the area, we were crushed. Eight years went by after the incident. After prayer and studying the Bible on the subject of love and forgiveness, we were prompted by the Holy Spirit to break down the wall of separation that stood between the two ministries.

God instructed us to give this ministry our church pews that had been recently refurbished. They had recently found a building to worship in, but they were in need of pews. Through our obedience in giving the pews, the walls of rejection, bitterness and anger were torn down, and relationships were restored between the two ministries. To God be the glory!

In many cases, God does not erase the memory of past hurts and disappointments from our minds; He lessens the pain of the memory. God gives us a way to escape the destruction of anger by showing us how to love those who have offended us. It is through our obedience that healing comes to our lives. Remember: Conflict does not mean an absence of love. Conflict is simply a signal that you need to find a workable solution. Resolve to be a good manager of your energy, relationships and anger.

Notes

Chapter 1
Anger: The Constructive and Destructive Emotion

1. *Vine's Expository Dictionary of Biblical Words* in PC Study Bible Version 3.1 (Seattle, Wash.: BibleSoft, 1993), s.v. "renew."
2. Information from the Mothers Against Drunk Driving national office in Irving, Tex.
3. Ibid.
4. *Vine's Expository Dictionary*, s.v. "anger."

Chapter 2
Righteous Indignation

1. *Nelson's Illustrated Bible Dictionary* in PC Study Bible Version 3.1 (Seattle, Wash.: BibleSoft, 1993), s.v. "wrath."

Chapter 4
Letting Off Steam Without Getting Burnt

1. *Vine's Expository Dictionary*, s.v. "bitterness."

Chapter 5
Do You Blow Up or Clam Up?

1. Audio Digest, Psychiatry, vol. 6:24, 1977.

2. David Glass, *Behavior Patterns, Stress and Coronary Disease* (Hillsdale, N.J.: Lawrence Erlbaum Associates, 1977), 26.
3. Ibid., 33.

Chapter 11
Learning to Count to Ten —
or to One Hundred

1. Barbara M. Bowen, *Strange Scriptures That Perplex the Western Mind* (Grand Rapids, Mich.: Wm. B. Eerdmans Publishing, 1944), 31-32.

Chapter 12
The Power of Gentleness

1. *Vine's Expository Dictionary*, s.v. "gentle, gentleness, gently."
2. Mack and Brenda Timberlake, *Lifesavers for Your Marriage* (Tulsa, Okla.: Harrison House, 1995), 58.
3. Mack and Brenda Timberlake, *Heaven on Earth in Your Marriage* (Tulsa, Okla.: Harrison House, 1993), 26.

ABOUT THE AUTHORS

Dr. Mack Timberlake, Jr. and Pastor Brenda Timberlake met during their college days and were married in December 1970. After twenty-five years of marriage, they have received a firsthand revelation that, with God at the center, marriage can be a joy.

As pastors and conference speakers, their insights into marriage and family have blossomed into a ministry that is shared with thousands around the world through different mediums. Pastors Mack and Brenda are contributing authors to *Living in the Real World* for *Charisma* magazine. Their national television program entitled *Mack and Brenda Timberlake* is aired on the Inspirational Network and other television stations. Also, they can be heard worldwide through various radio programs.

They pastor Christian Faith Center in Creedmoor, North Carolina, where more than five thousand people attend weekly. In 1995, they dedicated the first phase of "Baby Ark," which has a school, a twenty-eight-unit senior citizens' complex, a media department, a bookstore and a two-thousand-seat sanctuary.

Mack and Brenda are the parents of three

daughters, LaNica, Christanie and Majesty, and one son, Timothy. Their latest addition to the family is their adoptive niece, KáTiera. Together they are committed to one goal — taking this world for the Lord Jesus Christ.

If you enjoyed *I'm Mad About You,* then *A Christian's Survival Guide to Anger!* is a must.

Pastors Mack and Brenda Timberlake walk you through the Scriptures showing you how anger can become a stepping stone rather than a stumbling block. Whether you watch the ninety-minute video or listen to the four-tape audio series, you won't want to miss this blessing!

Books by Pastors Mack and Brenda Timberlake

Lifesavers for Your Marriage
$6

Lifesavers for Financial Freedom
$6

Heaven on Earth in Your Marriage
$8

What to Do When the Wine Runs Out in Your Marriage
$5

Audio & Video Series

When Pressure Is Pressing You (four-tape audio)
$20

Winning Over Bitterness (two-tape audio)
$10

Relate & Communicate (four-tape audio)
$20

How to Get the Devil Out of Your Family
(four-tape audio)
$20

Breaking the Spirit of Financial Stress
(three-tape audio)
$15

Building Bridges & Tearing Down Walls (video)
$20

You Can Love Again (video)
$20

You Can Love Again (four-tape audio)
$20

To order the audio and/or video series *A Christian's Survival Guide to Anger!* or for information about any of the products, contact:

Christian Faith Center
101 South Peachtree Street
Creedmoor, NC 27522
919-528-1581

If you enjoyed *I'm Mad About You*, we would like to recommend the following books:

Daddy Loves His Girls
by T. D. Jakes

Daddy Loves His Girls is the next step beyond T. D. Jakes' *Woman, Thou Art Loosed!* It explores the fatherly love God has for His daughters. It offers hope for women with painful pasts, and it gives men the courage to love their daughters.

Life Without Strife
by Joyce Meyer

Do you have a troubled relationship with a friend, family member or with somebody at church? If so, *Life Without Strife* exposes the root of strife in your life.

Out of Control and Loving It!
by Lisa Bevere

Out of Control and Loving It! is Lisa Bevere's journey from fearful, frantic control to a haven of rest and peace under God's control. It shows how to surrender your life, husband, children, finances, job or ministry to God.

Available at your local Christian bookstore or from:

Creation House
600 Rinehart Road
Lake Mary, FL 32746
1-800-283-8494
Web site: http://www.strang.com